Project Management

TRAINING

Includes CD-ROM with
Ready-to-Use Microsoft
PowerPoint™ Presentations

Exercises, Handouts, Assessments, and Tools
to Help You:

✔ Build Practical Project Management Training That
   Will Create an Organization of "Project-Oriented Thinkers"
✔ Develop Training for Both Individual
   and Organizational Needs
✔ Become a More Effective and Efficient Facilitator
✔ Ensure Training Is on Target and Gets Results

 ASTD Press

Bill Shackelford

Library of Congress Catalog Card Number: 2003113723

ISBN: 1-56286-364-9

Acquisitions and Development Editor: Mark Morrow

Copyeditor: Rick Ludwick, UpperCase Publication Services, Ltd.

Interior Design and Production: Christine Cotting, UpperCase Publication Services, Ltd.

Cover Design: Charlene Osman

Cover Illustration: Todd Davidson

The ASTD Trainer's WorkShop Series is designed to be a practical, hands-on road map to help you quickly develop training in key business areas. Each book in the series offers all the exercises, handouts, assessments, structured experiences, and ready-to-use presentations needed to develop effective training sessions. In addition to easy-to-use icons, each book in the series includes a companion CD-ROM with PowerPoint presentations and electronic copies of all supporting material featured in the book.

- ◆ *New Supervisor Training*
  John E. Jones and Chris W. Chen

- ◆ *Customer Service Training*
  Maxine Kamin

- ◆ *New Employee Orientation Training*
  Karen Lawson

- ◆ *Leading Change Training*
  Jeffrey Russell and Linda Russell

- ◆ *Leadership Training*
  Lou Russell

- ◆ *Coaching Training*
  Chris W. Chen

Contents

Chapter 4   DESIGNING YOUR PROJECT MANAGEMENT TRAINING   31

Chapter 5   FACILITATING YOUR PROJECT MANAGEMENT TRAINING   39

It's been said that a person with a hammer tends to see everything as a nail, but good craftspeople know that there's a tool for every job. Project management can provide a veritable Swiss army knife of tools that can prove useful in many different situations within your organization. Interest in project management as a discipline continues to grow, and the knowledge base within most organizations has grown accordingly. Project management works best when all of the parties involved in a project understand the basic tools and practices being used. No one can afford—or would even want—to certify everyone in the organization as a Project Management Professional. On the other hand, today's emphasis on doing more with less makes basic project management skills a must for almost every member of your organization.

Project management is many things to many people, but you are the training professional who can best determine who needs what level of project management training. This book offers some suggestions that may be helpful, but you alone are familiar enough with your organization's unique project management needs to create a training program that will have the greatest short-term and long-term benefits.

You may decide to use the workshops provided here "right out of the box," but you will more likely tailor each of them to fit the needs of your various audiences. However, you rarely should find it necessary to create a workshop from scratch and you will most likely find yourself mixing and matching materials and adding new modules that you can use both in current and future workshops.

The content of this book reflects more than 30 years' experience in project management, both as a practitioner and as a trainer. As a result, the list of people who have inspired and influenced me would fill a book of its own. There are, however, a few key individuals who have been major influences and whose ideas permeate much of what follows. I am forever indebted to

xii   ◆   **Preface**

Lou Russell and my fellow facilitators at Russell Martin & Associates for their ideas, enthusiasm, encouragement, and comradeship. Thanks as well to my fellow faculty members in the Project Management M.B.A. program of Keller Graduate School of Management of DeVry University, especially my colleague and mentor, Cathy Grogan.

Finally, I want to thank the Reverend Joette Waters, advisor Marsha Haake, and trusted friend John Sears for their ongoing inspiration and support throughout the writing the book.

Bill Shackelford
Chicago, Illinois
January 2004

Introduction: How to Use This Book Effectively

- A look at 12 common myths about project management

- Suggestions on how to make the most of the materials in this workbook

- A guide to what's included in the workbook and on the CD

The *art* of project management reaches back to prehistory: We still marvel that achievements ranging from Stonehenge to the Great Pyramids to the cathedral at Chartres to the Wright brothers' first successful flight in December 1903 were all created without the benefit of the formal tools and methods we now think of as part of the *science* of project management. So you might be asking, "Hey, if those folks didn't need it, why should we bother spending time and money training people in our organizations to be project managers?" Well, I think first of all that project management is *both* an art and a science. I also believe that both the science and the art are teachable, that people within organizations can benefit immediately from even small doses of project management knowledge, and that organizations can put together effective project management mini-curricula without incurring a lot of expense.

As an instructor in a graduate M.B.A. program in project management, I also hasten to add that we are talking in this book mainly about the teaching of introductory project management. Most of the training we'll be designing here will be for training events of a couple of days or less. Yes, project management by now has an extensive body of knowledge—with a small "b.o.k."

here; we'll discuss the Project Management Institute's *A Guide to the Project Management Body of Knowledge, 2000 Edition* (PMBOK) a little later on. We will focus on training in project management basics, but we will make sure to include essential material and pointers to "what's next?"

Everyone's a Project Manager

In the broadest terms, every person in your organization has at one time or another been faced with the job of planning and executing some sort of project. It might have been a simple thing like organizing a family picnic or something quite complex like developing a software application for one of your departments. Even though these two projects seem worlds apart in importance, objectives, and resource requirements, they have a great deal in common in terms of the planning and overseeing that will make them successes. (Since far more family picnics occur on schedule than software product launches, we might want to withhold judgment about which of the project managers involved has the most savvy!)

According to the 2000 PMBOK Guide, a project is "A temporary endeavor undertaken to create a unique product or service" (page 4). I think you'll agree that both putting together the family picnic and developing the software product qualify as projects. In fact, a good portion of our time at home and at work is devoted to projects. We may not always be in charge of every undertaking, but we very often wind up in supervisory or management roles in at least a few of them. Thus, whether we know it or not, we are already project managers. We've probably had some successes in these projects of which we are proud. In other cases, we may have an uneasy feeling that there might have been a better way to get the work done. It was this same vague uneasiness that eventually led to the development of project management as a discipline. It's always gratifying to see participants in project management training have their first "Aha!" experience when they encounter a tool or technique that they see will help them avoid repeating some painful experience they've had in past projects.

12 Common Myths about Project Management

There are just about as many ideas about what project management is all about as there are projects. If you are about to embark on a program of project management training, you should be aware of some of the common myths about project management so you can dispel them from the outset. Managing expectations is as big a part of project management training as it is of project management itself. So, here are my top 12 myths from the annals of project management mythology.

1. **Project management training will immediately result in all our projects coming in on time and within budget.** This is the number one training myth. Viewing any training program as a silver bullet is bound to end up with some disappointed participants and managers, so manage expectations carefully. When you do your training needs assessment with your internal customers, try to identify areas where your organization should see some immediate improvements. Make sure your expectations and your means of measuring results are realistic and verifiable. If your program is successful, you will eventually see improvements in project delivery and cost containment, but the process will take time—and plenty of fine-tuning by the project management teams as they gather and apply lessons learned.

2. **If you know how to use project management software, you know all you need to know about project management.** Project management software is a valuable tool for project managers, but project management is no more merely about software than home construction is merely about hammers. The training we'll be discussing does not require the use of project management software. I always insist on teaching project management concepts before running any kind of training on such software as Microsoft Project.

3. **Only people who will actually be working as project leaders need to learn project management.** The more we can train rank-and-file team members, project stakeholders, and subject matter experts called in to assist teams in understanding their assignments, the more successful we'll be in ensuring success by keeping the right individuals involved and informed. Keeping project management knowledge as the exclusive domain of team leaders and project managers can be an unfortunate mistake!

4. **Project management is mainly people management. ("I'm good with people, so I don't need to take project management training.")** Those who have a natural talent for motivating

and leading teams possess important skills that are required to be a first-rate project manager. However, failure to understand how to apply the tools and techniques of project management can doom a project—even ones under the direction of a charismatic project leader.

5. **A one-day or half-day project management course can't really teach anyone much about project management.** A project management neophyte can learn much in even a few hours of project management training, but you will need to carefully manage expectations and identify areas in which a little knowledge might be a dangerous thing. We'll address some of these areas as we introduce our training plans. For the most part, however, short introductory training can be very effective in raising awareness of project management within your organization and setting the stage for further development.

6. **We need to develop training to cover all levels of project management within our organization.** Let's get real! Unless you have virtually unlimited resources, try to keep your initial training efforts confined to the levels described in this book. You may later decide to expand a bit, perhaps developing a workshop that follows your organization's project management methodology or one that addresses an upcoming mega-project that is about to launch. If you have project office staff, you may provide even more advanced work in cooperation with them. Only the very largest organizations would decide to provide the higher levels of training that are available through a university, the Project Management Institute, or other organizations specializing in project management education. For now, consider starting small and building on your initial successes.

7. **Unless one is planning to go all the way and get certified as a Project Management Professional (PMP), studying project management is a waste of time.** Your organization may be seeking to have a number of PMPs on board. They certainly can be the catalysts for company-wide project management initiatives, and they will always maintain important roles as leaders and mentors for projects and teams in your organization. At the same time, I believe that in order to develop a true "project-oriented" organization, you will want as many staff as possible to have basic and intermediate project management skills.

8. **People who are involved in project management already will naturally be motivated to attend project management training.** *Au contraire,* I fear. Project managers may not necessarily feel they "know it all already," but many may feel they know enough to be bored or feel out of place in an introductory workshop. You'll want to have a plan for using the skills they bring to the table. Obtaining their assistance in the training can help you, and give them a stronger motivation for attending.

9. **Unless I include elaborate, expensive simulations in my training, students will not get a real "feel" for how project management works.** The simulations we'll include here will be simple and inexpensive—and often just as effective as the ones costing tens of thousands of dollars. Simulations are necessary for the most effective learning, but you don't need to be George Lucas to produce them.

10. **It is not possible to teach project management effectively online.** As a matter of fact, project management turns out to be an excellent topic for online learning. Project management learning requires hands-on experience, a dialogue with other learners, and ready access to course materials and other instructional resources. Online learning can provide all of these without having to set up elaborate synchronous Web meeting schedules.

11. **Since projects are unique by definition, it makes no sense to try to use common processes within the organization.** Too many organizations use this as an excuse not to standardize methods and procedures for managing projects. Your long-term organizational goal ought to be a common language spoken about projects and common forms and methods to administer most of them. We don't want to create a dogmatic "this is the only way" approach, but a flexible framework for defining and delivering projects and products.

12. **In planning project management training, we don't need to involve the project office or other owners of project management processes within the organization. After all, this is just basic training.** If you have these resources available in your organization, by all means contact them early in your course development planning. They will undoubtedly have

resources available that can assist you. But even more important will be their guidance and support in helping you make your training a part of the existing project management support structure. When possible, substitute real examples of forms and templates from the Project Office. Taking advantage of their assistance can give your courses a great deal more substance and credibility, as well as prevent you from "reinventing the wheel" when the time comes to expand your training program.

How to Make the Most of This Workbook

This book can serve as "training in a box" if you would like to use the ready-made training programs it presents. You'll find lesson plans, complete with suggested timings, handouts, PowerPoint slides, and instructions for activities for three project management training programs:

- ◆ Project Management Overview (half-day session, chapter 7)

- ◆ Project Management Jump-Start (full-day session, chapter 8)

- ◆ Project Management Essentials (two-day session, chapter 9)

Many of you will prefer to mix and match exercises and materials to meet specific training needs and schedules. The materials in the book and on the CD should make this relatively painless, because you'll find their designs simple enough to be customizable without undoing a great many fancy fonts or color schemes.

Here is a suggested approach to get the most out of the book:

- ◆ **Skim the book.** Take a few minutes to thumb through the entire book, noting the "What's in This Chapter?" section at the beginning of every chapter and familiarizing yourself with the overall organization of the chapters and where you'll find handouts, training instruments, and other artifacts used in the courses.

- ◆ **Read chapter 2, "Project Management for Everyone."** This chapter continues the discussion started in chapter 1 and provides a philosophical basis for conducting project management training within your organization.

- ◆ **Read chapter 3, "Getting a Reading on Your Project Management Training Needs," for some suggestions on how to**

assess the most pressing project management training needs. This chapter will help you develop both short-term and long-term project management strategies and partner with internal project management leaders to provide training that reflects current best practices within your organization.

◆ **Read chapters 4 through 6 to get an overview of the three remaining steps in preparing to deliver project management training.** Chapter 4 addresses the design of your training for diverse audiences with differing levels of expectation, time availability, and motivation. Chapter 5 is about facilitation techniques for both standup training and various "virtual" approaches. Chapter 6 suggests some realistic methods of evaluating your training to ensure continuous improvement.

◆ **Read chapters 7 through 9, to view three more or less complete training courses you can use as the starting point for creating your program.** Each of these chapters will refer you to learning modules (chapter 10), learning activities (chapter 11), and project management tools (chapter 12) that make up each of the four courses.

◆ **Customize your training as needed.** Once you've worked through the book, you'll be ready to decide how much or how little you want to tailor the materials to create your own training courses. You may wish to "brand" your version of the materials to customize your training by adding your company logo or substituting your own forms and terms where necessary. However, be sure to review the appendix regarding the adaptation of copyrighted materials.

◆ **Run your training.** You may want to start with a small pilot program to fine-tune your courses. Evaluate the pilot and be prepared to make adaptations as needed to stay on track.

◆ **Have fun!** Project management training can be one of the most enjoyable experiences a trainer can have. Project management training almost always turns on a good many "light bulbs" for participants even in a short course. The courses outlined here provide plenty of interaction and almost always enough "Aha!" experiences to keep your students engaged and enlightened.

What's in This Workbook and on the CD?

All the training materials, PowerPoint presentations, and accompanying handouts, forms, training instruments, and evaluation forms appearing in this workbook are included in the CD that accompanies this book. Follow the instructions in the Appendix, "Using the Compact Disc" and the document on the CD titled "How to Use This CD" to access the materials on the disc.

The training materials in this book and CD include:

- ◆ discussion of the importance of project management to people and organizations (chapter 2)

- ◆ guidance on identifying project management training needs (chapter 3)

- ◆ assistance in designing, facilitating, and evaluating your project management training (chapters 4 through 6)

- ◆ training workshops that can be used as is or modified in response to your organization, its challenges, and your own teaching style (chapters 7 through 9)

- ◆ training modules to be used during the workshops (chapter 10 and CD)

- ◆ handouts, learning activities, and training instruments that are designed to fit into the training modules (chapter 11 and CD)

- ◆ training instruments participants will fill out during training (chapter 12 and CD)

- ◆ Microsoft PowerPoint presentations and slides for your use in focusing the energy of workshop participants (CD)

- ◆ additional resources for future reference—including books and Websites that you may find helpful in designing effective training programs and in understanding project management.

Icons

For easy reference, icons are included in the margins throughout this workbook to help you quickly locate key elements in training design and instruction. Here are the icons and what they represent:

CD: Indicates materials included on the CD accompanying this workbook.

Clock: Indicates recommended timeframes for specific activities.

Discussion Questions: Highlights questions you can use to explore important issues as part of a training activity.

Handout: Indicates handouts that you can print or copy and use to support training activities.

Key Point: Alerts you to key points that you should emphasize as part of a training activity.

Learning Activities: Identifies where learning activities occur in an agenda.

PowerPoint Slides: Indicates PowerPoint presentations and slides that can be used individually. These presentations and slides are on the CD included with this workbook, and copies of the slides are included in chapters 6 through 9. Instructions for using PowerPoint slides and the CD are included in the Appendix, "Using the Compact Disk."

Training Instrument: Identifies specific tools, checklists, and assessments that are used before, during, and following the training workshop.

What to Do Next: Highlights recommended actions that you can take to make the transition from one section of this workbook to the next or from a specific training activity to another within a training module.

What to Do Next

- ◆ Review the next chapter for more about why project management training can help everyone in your organization.

- ◆ Consider what your target audiences should be for the training you develop.

- ◆ Talk over your assumptions with colleagues and see if they have additional ideas.

As you progress through the workbook and get ready to start designing your project management workshops, you may want to review some of the core texts on project management and make sure you have reference copies available as resources during course design and when you conduct the training. Take a look at the For Further Reading section at the end of this book for some recommendations. You may, of course, already have your favorite project management books, but check the additional sources to see if there's anything you think you might like to add.

Project Management for Everyone

- Minimizing the school-of-hard-knocks approach to learning project management

- Refusing to buy into the "We're too busy to plan" argument against project management training

- The value of project-oriented thinking and how project management training can help turn your organization into one filled with "project-oriented thinkers"

- How common tools and vocabulary can yield uncommon successes

In the last chapter, we said that almost everyone has played the role of project manager—either on the job or in part of their personal lives. Most people do remarkably well in managing projects, even though most of them have never thought of themselves as project managers or taken part in any kind of project management training. This means that a substantial part of effective project management must come from good old solid common sense. Because this is true, you can build on people's intuitive grasp of how to manage projects and teach them quite a bit about the discipline of project management in a relatively short time. This book encourages you to build on your audience's previous experience to help them add project management tools and best practices to their existing skills. If they have been successful with their projects, your goal is to see to it that they'll be even more successful when armed with the project management knowledge offered in your training program. If they have struggled trying to make projects succeed, your project management training program can offer solutions to the problems they experienced.

The Accidental Project Manager

Project management has sometimes been called the "accidental profession" because so many project managers take on their first project management duties without benefit of formal training. They often are promoted to these positions because they've succeeded as a software programmer or a salesperson or advertising designer or other nonmanagement role. They may have good social skills and even exhibit strong leadership potential. In other words, they seem to intuitively possess all of the requisite attributes of a good project manager. They lack only one key ingredient: project management skills.

Needless to say, these "accidental project managers" are in for a bumpy ride as they try to work through their first few projects. Many embark on a crash reading program to find help. Many also wisely seek out other project managers in the organization who have demonstrated some degree of success. They pick up tips and tools more or less randomly, often getting contradictory information about how best to plan and manage projects. They hear terminology that often changes from one area within the company to another. No one uses the same word to mean the same thing. It's the Tower of Babel project all over again.

The "No Time for Planning" Trap

Unfortunately, the "No Time for Planning" trap is one of the most prevalent reasons why many organizations hobble along for years before adopting an overall project management approach. The trap is easy to fall into, and—even more insidious—it's easy to get agreement from fellow hobblers that stopping to examine and improve existing processes is just too expensive a luxury in today's demanding world. Stephen Covey and others have shown time and again that balancing urgent and important tasks is essential to effectiveness. It takes courage and commitment to escape the trap of failing to plan, but the payoff for escaping is immeasurable.

The Project-Oriented Organization

Until recently, most organizations tended to specialize in a relatively small number of products and services. Today, almost every organization—from corporations to small businesses to not-for-profit organizations—faces the challenge of responding to constantly changing demands from their customers and clients. Older manufacturing and service models have given way to the project model, a model requiring new skills and paradigms. The project-oriented organization usually has most if not all of the following characteristics:

- **There is an ongoing mix (portfolio) of short-term and long-term activities centered on producing products and services.** In order to remain competitive and to meet rapidly changing needs of customers and clients, organizations engage in strategic planning to identify activities to increase revenue, reduce costs, improve services, keep pace with competitors, or comply with regulatory requirements. This portfolio continues to grow and will require pruning as time goes on. The projects that survive usually must be proven to align with the organization's overall mission and promise a good return-on-investment.

- **Instead of annual budgets, there are budgets dedicated to each initiative.** Each project generally will have its own budget and a project sponsor who negotiates funding approval for the undertaking. These budgets usually require both preliminary and final estimates based on an evolving picture of the project requirements.

- **There is a recognition of a need for repeatable processes for managing work in the organization.** At some point, it becomes clear that many initiatives have very similar sets of activities, reporting requirements, and problems. Organizations begin to see the advantage of standardizing their approach to projects. This is the true beginning of the project-oriented organization.

- **There is a preponderance of work involving multiple departments or lines of business.** Instead of being centered in one functional area of the organization, work almost always crosses departmental lines and requires collaboration among several different areas. Individuals needed for the work frequently report to different line managers who make staff available to the project but who maintain authority over them. The project manager's authority is more or less secondary to that of the line manager.

- **There is a recognition of the need for a common vocabulary for communicating with internal and external customers.** Because multiple initiatives are under way, with many of their participants widely distributed within the organization, it becomes increasingly necessary to have consistent terminology and approaches to defining goals, objectives, and deliverables; performing tasks; reporting progress; and dealing with risks and changes of scope. Without a common vocabulary, customers inside and outside the organization are likely to become frustrated in their dealings with the new initiatives as they come along. Consistency in approach and definition of terms helps keep everyone "on the same page"—both within the organization and outside—in communicating with clients and customers.

- **There is a commitment to developing leadership skills throughout the organization.** Project-oriented organizations realize that leadership is just as important as technical skills and familiarity with project management tools and techniques. The ideal project manager is one who knows how to lead and inspire, how to negotiate and resolve conflict, how to spur groups to become high-performance teams. Project management programs in these organizations emphasize not only the mechanics of program management but also the so-called "soft skills."

- **There is a commitment to continuous improvement of project delivery: on time, under budget, and according to specification.** Organizations that are truly committed to continuous improvement recognize the need for consistent approaches to projects that use common ways of measuring progress and capturing lessons learned not only at the end of every initiative but also throughout the entire project delivery process. As lessons learned inform new projects, project teams measure success not only in terms of meeting objectives within defined schedules and budgets but also in terms of achieving greater efficiencies compared with previous project work. They also continually look at their current methods of project delivery to see where they might improve their general approach. Best practices become the starting point but become redefined as even *better* practices emerge.

Common Tools, Common Vocabulary, Exceptional Results

If your organization is a project-oriented organization—or is in the process of becoming one—you may already have developed methods and procedures and defined terms that you'll want used consistently throughout each project. If you are just starting with project management, you'll want to develop a basis for a common approach to projects and to the content you teach in your project management training. In this book, you'll find terms and approaches that reflect those recommended by the Project Management Institute and found in *A Guide to the Project Management Body of Knowledge, 2000 Edition* (often referred to as "the PMBOK"—pronounced "pimbock"). If you have not already adopted methods and terms, then the PMBOK would definitely be the logical place to start. But it is most important that all those involved in projects within your organization use terminology and approaches consistently. When this happens, you'll begin to see a number of important benefits:

◆ **Project teams and customers do not have to learn procedures and new jargon with each new project.** Surprisingly, this happens a lot more often than you'd think. One of the biggest drains on project schedules is the famous "learning curve." Many parts of projects, because they are unique, will require some degree of new learning; but it is a massive waste to have to learn new project life cycles, forms, tracking tools, review processes, and other project management approaches that could be standardized across the organization.

◆ **It becomes easier to compare projects over time when they involve similar measurements and approaches.** Ordinarily, no two projects are exactly alike; but many are sufficiently similar that having everyone use a similar approach will make it easier to obtain valuable lessons by evaluating a project against previous ones. Teams learn to repeat practices that worked well in certain phases of the project and avoid those that didn't work in others. Estimating becomes more accurate as historical data begins to accumulate based on a consistent set of definitions and measurements.

- **Consistent tracking and reporting helps uncover inefficiencies in the overall project management approach.** Locking in procedures may be helpful at first to achieve consistency across the organization, but you may soon discover flaws in the process that require changing those procedures. Adhering to inefficient procedures for too long is a common pitfall, so it's important to balance consistency with careful observation and an openness to correct faulty processes when you spot them. Repeatable processes evolve over time and projects.

These considerations have significant implications for your project management training efforts:

- Start out with the best possible approaches and terminology available, whether they are developed internally or adopted from generally accepted best practices.

- Make sure that training emphasizes the continuous improvement aspects of a solid project management initiative. Emphasize the importance of project reviews and lessons learned rather than merely teaching them as postscripts.

- Realize that whatever training you create must be flexible enough to change with your processes. Keep lines of communication open with those who will be observing and adapting the processes being adopted.

If you follow these principles, your training effort will balance consistency and flexibility and reflect continuously improving practices in your organization.

 ## What to Do Next

- Review notes taken when you talked with training colleagues in other organizations about their approach to project management training (as was recommended in this section of the preceding chapter).

- Skim chapter 3, "Getting a Reading on Your Project Management Training Needs," to help identify the most likely target audiences for your project management training.

◆ Read chapter 3, "Getting a Reading on Your Project Management Training Needs," in detail—taking notes to prepare for your project management training needs assessment.

◆ Thumb quickly through chapters 4 through 6 to get a feel for where you'll be going after you've done a training needs assessment based on your reading in chapter 3.

◆ ◆ ◆

The next chapter guides you through what may be one of the biggest challenges in putting together a project management training program: getting a needs assessment that truly reflects the gaps to be filled by project management training in your organization. The most important reminder is to overcome perfectionism. You are very likely to get differing views on training needs and differing ideas of the scope of your training project. Proceed with caution, but keep moving.

◆

Getting a Reading on Your Project Management Training Needs

What's in This Chapter?

- Ways to avoid "analysis paralysis"

- Ways to identify real project management training needs

- How to partner with the project office; what to do if you don't have one

- How to define and manage the scope of your project management training effort

- How to find your project management "angels"

- How to identify absolute versus relative success factors

- How to set short-term and long-term training goals

- How to plan ahead to demonstrate return-on-investment

- Ways to gather information

- How to report your findings

By now it may be clear that project management training can be of great benefit to your organization. Establishing common tools, practices, and terminology can help everyone involved in projects communicate better, work more efficiently, and apply lessons learned to future projects. A program of project management training can help prepare everyone who works on projects to use the same tools, apply the same practices, and communicate in a common language. How you define this program will determine its scope and help you draw a blueprint for your organization's training effort—for now and for the future.

Avoiding Analysis Paralysis

Getting started with a project management training effort can be a daunting undertaking. The pressure to get training out to the troops may be so great that you could easily fall into the trap of launching a series of workshops without first determining what your organization really needs.

However, another equally insidious pitfall is spending so much time analyzing your situation that the workshops will arrive too late to address your immediate training needs. Balance is everything. To deliver effective just-in-time training you'll need to do just-enough needs analysis. My only suggestion to perfectionists: Get over it! You are a professional and will know not to push a half-baked program out the door, so trust your ability to make an adequate project management training needs analysis within a carefully set time constraint.

Identifying Real Needs

As you begin your project management training needs assessment, don't be surprised if you encounter a mixture of resistance, indifference, constructive helpfulness, and—sometimes worse than resistance—overzealous enthusiasm. Your difficult task is to sort out sometimes conflicting information and come up with an accurate composite picture of your organization's project management training needs. As you proceed through this needs analysis, you'll want to manage the expectations of those with whom you are consulting in order to avoid premature assumptions about what your training program will look like and what it is trying to accomplish. Here are some considerations for each of the types of people you'll likely run into as you conduct your analysis:

- ◆ **Resisters.** Resisters are usually the way they are because they have fallen into the "No Time for Planning" trap. To them, project management training looks like nothing more than one more demand on their overfull schedules. It might be tempting to dismiss their input from your needs analysis, but listen carefully to their complaints. At this early stage, you are more interested in coming up with a complete statement about the current state of project management in the organization. The resisters may not see training as a solution to the problem, but they can give you insight into what gaps need to be filled.

◆ **"So what?" people.** These people may not actively resist the idea of project management training, but they also don't see any particular value in it and may be skeptical that training can change the current situation. Again, listen carefully to their observations. Ask probing questions—lots of "Why do you suppose that's the case?" questions—to help get to some root causes of their skepticism. Ask them if previous training efforts have failed and, if so, why. Ask them if they could picture any kind of scenario in which training could help. What would get *them* to want to come to a project management workshop; what would it look like?

◆ **Helpful people.** Love them. Nurture them. Protect them. Recommend them for promotions. Write thank-you letters to them. Send them flowers and candy. These folks are worth their weights in gold. You would like *all* of the participants in your needs analysis to be like this group, but in the real world there will probably be only a handful of individuals who 1) have a good understanding of the overall goals and of the organization, 2) are familiar with the current state of project management practice within your organization and can help you identify gaps between desired behavior and current practices, 3) are willing to answer questions throughout the needs analysis process, and—not required but desirable—4) know something themselves about project management.

◆ **Overzealous people.** You might call this group "helpful people on steroids." They can suddenly inflate your planned two-day workshop into an international symposium or your three-workshop series into a Ph.D. program. Very often, these people are looking for opportunities to expand their own learning (a good thing) but often are less interested in the real project management training needs of the organization (a bad thing). Your challenge will be to harness their energies and manage their expectations so you can get the most accurate picture of what's really needed. Be open to their ideas, but triangulate frequently by verifying their observations and stated needs through conversations with others in your organization. Again, we are initially trying to get a good statement of the training gap and identify possible ways to address it. Their suggestions may eventually turn out to be useful. Just don't let them force your hand so that you make promises that are unrealistic or that lead to training offerings that serve only a small handful of individuals within your organization.

The Project Office: Its Important Role (and What to Do if You Don't Have One)

One of the changes to the 2000 edition of the PMBOK Guide was to acknowledge the role of the project office. The acknowledgment is brief but helpful, stating that the project office's functions can range from simply "providing support functions to project managers in the form of training, software, templates, etc." (section 2.3.4., p. 21). all the way up to the actual management of projects. If you have a project office in your organization, they very likely will be your first stop as you perform your project management training needs assessment. (In fact, you probably have already been talking with them.) They often will have materials, templates, forms, and numerous other resources that will likely find their way into your workshop materials. They may also have done extensive needs analysis regarding training and will certainly have their finger on the pulse of the organization with respect to current project management training needs. The project office will be your primary source of information and your most resonant sounding board for training ideas. Count your blessings if you have this resource at your disposal.

If you do not have a project office, you'll need to find an alternative process for standardizing your organization's project management methods. The ideal solution will be to create a "virtual project office" consisting of some of your best existing project managers. These managers can act as a body to approve training materials and, if possible, adopt some standard practices to use as a starting point for introducing training for a project-oriented approach. Ideally, this virtual office should have the blessing and support of upper management and may eventually give way to a real brick-and-mortar project management office. For now, however, you are mainly interested in having an advisory group to help ensure that your project management needs assessment accurately reflects the organization's true needs and that your workshops will have the greatest potential for success.

Defining the Scope of Your Project Management Training Effort

The greatest threat to the success of any project (including your project to teach project management) is scope creep. We all intuitively understand this concept and its implications. However, for our purposes, it may be helpful to look at some of the dimensions of scope so we can better define our training project scope and manage the expectations of our training stakeholders.

◆ **Levels of material taught.** Are you merely providing a simple project management overview for new project team members? Are you providing a project management fundamentals workshop that will last a few days? People's definitions of even something as basic as "fundamentals" will vary widely, so you will need to get fairly precise course objectives established early in order to predict the time and effort required to develop and deliver the training.

◆ **Location of learners.** Are there multiple locations at which the workshops must be delivered? If the learning audience is widespread geographically, is there any possibility of delivering the training using e-learning or some blended approach that combines e-learning and live workshops?

◆ **Number of learners to receive the training.** If most of the training will be in an instructor-led workshop, the number of potential learners will have a direct cost on the time and materials needed to deliver the training. On the other hand, large numbers of trainees may be a cue to pursue e-learning or a blended approach.

Identifying Your Project Management "Angels"

Broadway producers call their financial backers "angels," patrons who believe in the potential for the planned production and who are willing to provide support and act as benevolent guiding influences. In your project management training effort, you too will need a few angels—some to sponsor and fund the undertaking and some to provide a benevolent guiding influence and mentor you as you prepare to roll out your first workshop. Angels show up in unexpected places, so don't be surprised to find some of your most valuable sources of ideas and guidance outside the normal lines of the org chart. Of course, start by looking for angels in a few of the most likely spots:

◆ **Your HR department.** HR staff are likely to find additional audiences for your training, share findings from earlier training needs analysis surveys, and provide you with access to tools and products that you might otherwise have to obtain on your own.

◆ **The project office.** These people will certainly be key supporters of your effort and can help bring you into contact with other members of the organization who can lend support and offer suggestions.

◆ **Departmental directors.** They may already feel such a great need for your planned offerings that they may be willing to help fund the project or at least commit to enrolling their staff in your workshops once they are available.

◆ **Star project managers.** They know how to do it and most likely can help you better communicate how to do it. If you don't have a project office, project managers are setting the *de facto* standards for best practices and can share some of their best ideas to incorporate in your project management training.

◆ **Training associates outside the organization.** At first you may think that these individuals would be limited in their roles to those of mentors for your projects. But don't overlook the possibility that they too may have an interest in your undertaking and might even contribute funding, time, and talent.

◆ **Prior workshop participants.** These individuals can be vital sources of information about what kinds of training have worked best in your organization. Their input can be revelatory; some may be candid enough to let you know the things they *haven't* liked. Getting feedback from a representative sampling of previous workshop participants almost always gives you useful perspectives on how to plan your next training initiatives.

◆ **Potential new workshop participants.** This group will have their own ideas about what they expect from project management training. Because they are going to be your frontline audience, understanding, managing, and—when possible—meeting their expectations should always be a primary consideration in planning your training. Learn all you can about their preferred learning styles (for example, lecture, hands-on exercises and simulations, offline reading, online interactive) and try to find a blend of delivery approaches that will be compatible with the majority of the group's preferences. When there are wide discrepancies in preferences, you may even want to consider alternative delivery methods for different types of learners.

Defining Absolute and Relative Project Management Training Success Factors

Even if you have full endorsement to proceed with your project training effort, you will want to start as soon as possible to target not only training objectives but also other factors that will satisfy those objectives. Training success is not just delivering a set of dynamite workshops that your participants adore (though this is a good start), it is also meeting other important objectives, often within such specified constraints as time, numbers of participants, or level of training delivered. Other success factors may be desired outcomes related to the training that are less easily quantifiable but are also desirable. We sometimes refer to these constraints as absolute and relative success factors.

Some examples of absolute success factors:

- ◆ We must train all 250 programmers and analysts in the IT department before November 10.

- ◆ Total costs of training cannot exceed $60,000, including travel expenses.

- ◆ All students must complete the preliminary overview training. All product developers must also receive the detailed scheduling and cost estimating modules.

Examples of relative success factors:

- ◆ Participants will have a variety of options for participating in the training, resulting in the fewest disruptions to work schedules.

- ◆ Participants may review materials online after the training in a facilitated refresher session.

- ◆ Participants may "test out" of the overview, using a prescreening test administered online.

As you can see, the relative success factors might in some organizations become absolute requirements; your needs analysis will verify which training elements must be included and which are "nice to have."

Short-Term and Long-Term Training Goals

In addition to determining the absolute and relative success factors for your project management training program, you'll want to establish a plan for delivering training that takes into account both the immediate, most pressing training needs and the long-term needs for staff development in project management. The materials in this workbook can provide the basis for general entry-level project management training workshops and are designed to get you up and running quickly. They may be adequate to meet your short-term needs, but over the longer term you may be required to provide more advanced training as well as continuing to offer the entry-level content to new staff. Use your needs assessment interviews to place priorities on training needs so that your first workshop offerings address the most pressing needs, and, at the same time, develop a plan for subsequent offerings that address long-term and continuing training needs.

Planning Ahead to Demonstrate ROI

At this stage of your needs analysis, it may be premature to attempt to prove ROI (return-on-investment) on your initial workshop offerings. Nevertheless, it is never too early to start thinking about the kinds of measures that might apply when it comes time to evaluate your rollout of project management training. During your needs analysis, begin asking those you interview about the ways they would measure success of the training.

- ◆ What kinds of savings might result from staff with improved project management skills and knowledge?

- ◆ Are there historical or current project data providing measurements that might be used as benchmarks?

- ◆ Are there ways of capturing data after the training is completed so that your organization can continue with the comparison?

- ◆ What would those you consult consider respectable improvement levels?

Obtaining as many ideas as you can will help you demonstrate the value of the training. The outset of your training effort may not be the time to attempt using financial models, but the ideas you pick up at this stage can help later when it's time to do so.

Methods of Information Gathering

Keeping in mind my the original caveat about analysis paralysis, you still would like to gather as much information as you can in order to define the most important objectives for your project management training. You've by now assembled quite a list of project management "angels" as well as a few individuals who can provide some candid advice about what you need to avoid. In some cases, you'll have specific people in mind; in others, you may simply want a representative sample of certain types of individuals (such as past participants, potential new trainees, and a cross-section of current project team members). In obtaining input from such a wide variety of individuals, you may want to expedite matters through a few frequently used surveying techniques:

◆ **In-person one-on-one interviews.** These sessions are invaluable for getting certain types of information and may be almost mandatory for some of your key stakeholders (your project sponsor or members of the project office, for example). All of the people in this category are likely to be very pressed for time. Start early to identify those you need to visit in person, begin inventorying the questions you need answered, and schedule your appointments as soon as you can.

◆ **Focus groups or other facilitated group meetings.** These meetings allow you to obtain feedback from as many as a dozen or so individuals at once. By having standardized questions and someone to record the proceedings, you can quickly gather a great deal of information in a short time. Some focus groups leaders videotape the meeting to capture facial expressions, gestures, and full-length spoken responses. Reviewing these can be extremely time-consuming; so you may prefer the technique whereby a designated recorder writes on flipcharts key points made during the proceedings so that all participants can see what is recorded. This helps keep people (literally) "on the same page" and may be the most efficient technique for requirements gathering you are doing.

◆ **Email or Internet surveys.** These instruments have the advantage of allowing you to compile statistics based on responses to a relatively small number of questions. They usually take much less participant time and may even be submitted anonymously. On the other hand, because they tend to be fairly "low-touch" you are not as likely to get the same kinds of insights that face-to-face meetings usually elicit.

◆ **Telephone interviews.** Phone interviews give you much greater flexibility in covering major issues surrounding the training than using questionnaires and surveys. Even though you don't have the advantage of reading body language over the phone, you can pick up a great deal of information from voice inflection and other cues from your interviewee.

◆ **Conference calls.** These can sometimes substitute for group sessions but have the disadvantage of having only an audio element. Whereas one-on-one telephone conversations can still provide considerable nonverbal feedback, as mentioned above, conference calls often lose momentum (and participants) due in part to the "sensory deprivation" of having only disembodied voices to sustain interest. If you decide to use conference calls as a means of gathering information, be sure to provide each participant with a written agenda, handouts, and other materials to keep the discussion focused.

◆ **Online chat.** These are the online equivalent of conference calls and have many of the same pitfalls. They too require that participants be available at the same time to interact.

◆ **Online real-time group meetings.** These meetings combine the advantages of the focus group with some of the convenience of telephone conference calls. Here however, participants usually focus on materials presented online and can interact in chat, Q&A, and other methods while the meeting is in progress.

◆ **Online newsgroups or threaded discussions.** Because these forums use online bulletin boards for posting and responding to questions, viewing handouts and other resources, and are accessible from anywhere there is Web access, they offer several advantages:

    ◆ Participants do not have to be available at the same time.

    ◆ The meeting interactions are self-documenting.

    ◆ The discussion can include numerous subtopics, allowing meeting participants to involve themselves in as many or as few of the subtopics as is appropriate.

Reporting Your Findings and Getting Approval

Once you've finished your interviews, you will need to take some time to digest the information obtained, hold follow-up sessions with your key stakeholders, and make your final recommendations. Compare your current understanding of the overall project management needs with your available training resources and target the gap between them. To what extent will the basic materials here (and perhaps anything already available in your organization) require adaptation or supplementation? What resources appear to be needed to fill that gap? What can you deliver within a short timeframe? What may need to be postponed?

Answering these questions will form the basis of your preliminary report. This report should seek approval to proceed to a more detailed cost and time estimate. If it is approved, you will need to review the absolute and relative success factors that you've uncovered. Normally your project sponsors will appreciate having a range of numbers to choose from, starting with the solution that addresses all of the absolute training requirements and moving to a set of alternate estimates that embrace some or all of the relative success factors. Once you have gotten this far, you will be ready to start your training design in earnest.

What to Do Next

- ◆ Put together your "short list" of project management "angels."

- ◆ Determine the best combination of ways to obtain information from each person on the list; for example, one-on-one, focus group, or virtual online meeting.

- ◆ Read chapters 4 through 6 carefully and take notes to prepare for your meetings. Remember, the people you meet are going to have questions for you as well.

- ◆ Pretend for a moment that the training design is complete as you read chapter 6 and outline the questions that your workshop evaluations should ask. Be prepared to review these possible questions with those you're interviewing. Listen carefully for any concerns they may have that could be addressed by questions on the evaluation.

◆ ◆ ◆

In chapter 4, you'll get started with preliminary course design, basing your overall approach on the outcomes of your needs analysis. You'll see how to map these findings to an overall curriculum plan for your project management training effort. Curriculum and course design is usually an iterative process, so don't be surprised to find yourself roughing out some working prototypes for your training (using resources available in this book) and then returning to this chapter to revisit some of the needs assessment steps. This approach can help you arrive at a training solution that truly reflects your organization's needs.

Designing Your Project Management Training

- How to target your training to a wide audience

- Ways to match your training styles to learner preferences

- How to implement your short-term and long-term training goals

- How to craft an effective project management curriculum

- How to scale the training to accommodate hectic schedules

- How to deliver speed-of-light training with a project management e-course

Now that you've completed your project management training needs analysis, you may at first feel as though you are suffering from information overload. You may also be wondering if perhaps you should continue your research a while longer. Don't let analysis paralysis set in at this late date. It's time to put together a project management training program based on what you've learned. You have already planned to gather lessons learned, and chances are you'll gather quite a few the first time around. That's why you may want to run a pilot workshop or two before announcing a massive training rollout. Plan to start small and adapt as necessary to create a program that meets the needs of your organization.

Targeting a Wide Audience

Don't be surprised if your first request for project management training comes from one specialized area within your organization. Because complex, specialized assignments and projects can surface in any business area, a group may suddenly realize that their staff needs project management skills in a hurry. As you work with them, you begin to discover that some of their training may have to address their specific practices and may even need to use some of their specialized vocabulary. Time pressures may tempt you to give up the big picture of planning an organization-wide project management training program, but try to hold your ground and simultaneously focus on your long- and short-term goals. Separate the universal from the specific as much as possible so that you can develop your training in "chunks" that can be redeployed in later project management training workshops. Even though it may seem counterintuitive at the moment, this disciplined, modular approach will pay off in greater rather than less flexibility.

In planning your training, strive for:

◆ **Modularity.** Plan learning activities that are as self-contained as possible. These can then be placed in a variety of learning contexts. For instance, a simple exercise may be appropriate for a short overview session and as part of an intermediate workshop. Rather than creating a long multiple-section document containing handouts and other learning resources, keep each item as a separate file so it can be compiled into any number of different learning aids.

◆ **Reusability.** The principle of reusability means that your learning modules should avoid including such data as date, workshop name, or even page numbers whenever possible. These elements can be added at the time a specific workshop "goes to press." The added time you spend today in separating this data from the substantive learning content will pay off many times over when you are able to incorporate the same module in another workshop with little or no modification

◆ **Adaptability.** Once you have achieved reusability, the next level for which to strive is adaptability of course content. Plan content so you can expand or condense presentation material to fit different learning needs and different time slots. In this book, you'll find some of the same materials in the half-day overview that you'll find in the two-day course. Whenever possible think in terms of how a piece of course content can be juxtaposed with related materials in other courses to create customized versions for your learning customers. Over time, you'll become increasingly adept at this valuable skill and will be able to quickly assemble custom materials from course content you've already developed.

♦ **"Findability."** I have a large collection of computer data, audio recordings, and videotapes that have accumulated over the years. The only problem is that when the time comes to access a file, listen to an opera, or watch an old movie, I far too often spend long periods searching for my targeted item, all the while saying "There it is!" to dozens of things I thought I'd lost forever. Despite vows to the contrary, I'm very bad at organizing and labeling personal media. Fortunately, I've learned to do a better job with the materials I use for training. As a zealous convert, I want to recommend that you do everything possible to organize your course materials so you can find everything required and reuse and adapt the modules when you're developing a new course or workshop.

Applied Learning Theory 101: Matching Delivery to Learning Preferences

Remember that you are targeting a wide audience and that your participants will have widely different preferences for how they acquire knowledge. To the extent you can, try to appeal to as many of these preferences as possible.

♦ **Slides and materials.** The PowerPoint files included in this book are intentionally minimalist in design. Too many workshops consist of an endless series of densely filled slides that are both difficult to read and tedious to try to cover in a classroom setting. Some of your audience will not mind this sort of presentation, but most will find such workshop formats intolerable. For your visual learners, have handouts or additional reading lists available, but keep your workshop materials simple and concentrated on your key learning objectives.

♦ **Lecture, discussion, and debriefing.** Your interaction with the class is in many ways a dialogue wherein you and your participants exchange ideas and solve problems relating to their project management learning needs. This is the place where you turn the workshop into a living experience, as you relate the materials and activities to the experiences and concerns of your learners. As with everything else about training, balance is everything. If you do not add this valuable component to the workshop, it will remain more or less a "canned" presentation. On the other hand, if you allow discussions to drag out endlessly or subject your learners to "death by lecture," you will have destroyed all the potential benefits of dialogue. The suggested timings for the workshops in this book reflect my belief that presentations, lectures, and discussions need to be carefully timed to maintain learner interest and maximize the impact of each verbal interaction.

◆ **Individual activities.** Students need time to think and work individually to better process at least some of learning content in your workshops. In some cases, these needs may be met with simple questionnaires that allow participants to provide background information that can help you better facilitate the workshop. In others, participants will be working through a series of questions that will help prepare them for an upcoming discussion or a shared small group activity. Still others may be individual exercises, self-assessments, or puzzles that allow practice of new skills acquired in the workshop. Your biggest challenge with these activities lies in the fact that people tend to work at different paces and you don't want to have some participants finishing an exercise early and having to wait for the slower individuals to finish. For this reason, the individual exercises in this book have intentionally been kept short so you can more easily pace your workshop participants. If you add individual exercises to those in the book, you may want to follow the same practice. And, once again, it will be important to include an ample number of individual exercises but not have so many that your workshop begins to look like a study hall. Just as important, you will want to have a debriefing or small group discussion after each of these exercises. In the workshops in this book, you'll find several sequences of individual learning activities that lead to small group discussion or exercise and end with a general debriefing for the entire group.

◆ **Small-group activities.** The small group activities in workshops often are where your participants have the greatest opportunity to practice new skills and reinforce learning through team interaction. Collaborative activities help your participants to learn and fill in the gaps for one another in applying newly acquired concepts and tools. Small-group activities present an especially difficult challenge to you as a facilitator—even more than the one presented by individual activities. Timing will be important to make certain all groups stay "on the same page" in working through an exercise or case study.

Your debriefing of these activities will be especially critical to the success of the activities in particular and to the workshop in general. Don't be surprised to find groups differing in their conclusions, and try as much as possible to capitalize on the differences as a springboard for in-depth discussion of the various issues raised. If you do this well, you will turn your workshop into a true forum for the exchange of ideas and make it much more relevant to your participants.

Through a judicious mix of these four major elements, you will go a long way toward meeting the various needs of your learning audience, whether their primary learning style involves reading, listening, or doing (individually and in groups).

Revisiting Short-Term and Long-Term Training Goals

In the preceding chapter, you examined long- and short-term project management training goals. If you are very lucky, the workshop materials in this book may just about meet all of your short-term training goals. In reality, you may find that you'll need to adapt the workshops outlined here to include necessary additional content to meet some of your short-term goals, perhaps deferring or eliminating some content as not applicable. In adapting workshop content, keep in mind the element's modularity, reusability, adaptability, and "findability" discussed in the earlier section on "Targeting a Wide Audience."

Begin to think about the implications of your long-term training goals. Which ones are you going to address in the future? Which ones will you address with the help of an outside solution provider or training partner? Which ones will you leave to your individual learners to reach (perhaps through external workshops or a college course)? Examining these questions can help lead you to your first pass at a comprehensive project management training plan.

Crafting an Effective Project Management Curriculum

Like many development projects, putting together a project management training curriculum is an iterative process. As the time approaches to present your first project management workshops, these course offerings will be—for the time being, at least—fairly fixed; and you will be able to publish course outlines and syllabuses that accurately reflect the substance of these courses. Looking farther into the future, the course outlines may be less well-defined. You may even be tempted to post course outlines that imply that these courses are "waiting in the wings" to be offered on demand. Avoid leaving this impression if possible. Let your audience know that the outlines are tentative (not necessarily a bad thing at all, because you may very often hear requests to modify them). Indicate for each listing that the course is "under consideration," "under development," or some other characterization that accurately reflects its current status. Once you start to publicize your project management curriculum plan, you will almost certainly receive feedback that will help guide you to changes. The pressures of delivering your current crop of workshops may take up much of your time and energy at the beginning, but even then you will want to put aside time to hone your curriculum plan so you can stay on target in meeting long-term needs.

Scaling the Training to Accommodate Hectic Schedules

"We want a comprehensive project management workshop to teach the entire PMBOK, and we'd like to do it in one six-hour class." Hmmmmmm, sound familiar? (Actually, in one case it was one four-hour class!) As you begin to develop your project management workshops, you will almost certainly encounter requests for compressed timeframes. We are in a world where everyone expects to do more with less. Balance your desire to meet your training audience's schedule constraints with the realities of what you can actually deliver. If time is the most critical element, you may need to bargain for scaled-down learning objectives, alternative delivery methods, or a "mini-series" approach consisting of several half-day sessions each focused on some aspect of project management. Unless you have powerful high-level management support (and enforcement) of your training effort, beware of approaches that assume homework or other off-site effort by participants. Far too often, participants arrive with the homework unread, unexamined, or unfinished. You may even hear the modern version of "my dog ate it": "a virus corrupted it." Generally, you'll obtain better results by having the work done within the timeframe of the workshop.

Project Management Training at the Speed of Light: Creating a Project Management E-Course

If you think this section seems to contradict the warning given in the preceding section, you are correct. Many organizations introduce e-learning courses in project management, often purchased from one of the big e-learning vendors. The effectiveness of such courses depends entirely on the motivation of the student and usually excludes the valuable team interactions that occur in the types of workshops modeled in this workbook. In effect, these courses are automated versions of the "individual activities" discussed earlier in this chapter. Many do provide a type of debriefing in the form of feedback to the student but without the kind of interchange that occurs in a live workshop. Essentially the student works alone without interaction with others, precluding the kinds of collaborative learning that lectures and discussion and small-group activities afford.

E-learning courses have proven to be quite effective, although participants must be motivated to complete the course, and as with most training activities, management support will be essential.

What to Do Next

- ◆ Revisit your audience. Take time to review what you know about your audience and what you may have previously discovered about their learning preferences. After doing that, scan the activities in the three workshops outlined in chapters 7 through 9 to see if the mix of lectures, discussions, and individual and group activities would work effectively with your audience. Note where you may need to modify or augment.

- ◆ Half-hour speed drill. Take a piece of paper and sketch out on one page the project management workshops you would envision as part of your project management curriculum once it is completely in place. Put a checkmark beside the workshops you must have in place right away. Put a plus sign beside the workshops you'd like to introduce right away. Draft fairly detailed outlines for the "right away" items. Draft a high-level outline for your round two items. Indicate workshops you plan to develop internally, which ones you'll outsource, and which ones you'll let your target audience find on their own through external sources or through formal course work at a college or university campus. Keep this list and begin to refine it as the first steps toward a comprehensive project management training curriculum.

◆ Time-commitment readiness check. Get a reading of how many of your anticipated audience can be expected to participate in two-day workshops. If this timeframe is too long for many, do some brainstorming with colleagues in your organization to come up with alternative ways of delivering the same materials. Can you do it, for example, on consecutive Mondays or Mondays spaced two weeks apart? What activity or activities might need to be introduced to serve as a refresher when participants return for the second day? How realistic would homework be? Is there sufficient management support to ensure that homework actually would get done outside of class?

◆ E-learning readiness check. It's not too early to examine what you have available and consider offering an e-learning project management course. Meet with your IT or Web development group to discuss what it might take to implement such a course. Even if you decide not to offer an e-learning course now, it's good to get an overview of your current readiness to deliver one.

◆ ◆ ◆

Throughout this chapter, you've seen reference to the value of interactivity though discussions, debriefing, and team activity. In chapter 5, you'll see how your role as facilitator makes real learning possible as you guide students through a variety of learning activities. As you lead them, you'll be highlighting key learning points, creating shared understanding of the implications of the workshop's activities, and managing the flow of activities as you resolve or minimize conflicts and personality differences.

Facilitating Your Project Management Training

What's in This Chapter?

- How to define your role as a facilitator of project management learning

- Why facilitated project management training is more effective than other alternatives

- How collaborative learning supports and augments the project management training effort

- How facilitation can be effective in three different methods of project management training

- How to anticipate and manage problem situations and problem students

Now that you have largely determined the content and format of your first project management workshop offerings, it's time to start looking at what may be the single most important success factor for your training effort. A skilled facilitator needs to make the materials come alive so the participants can master the content and apply it once the workshops are over. Facilitation is much more than mere presentation of course materials. A facilitator leads workshop participants to a shared understanding of key concepts, helps each learner find relevance and applicability in the knowledge gained, and leaves each individual with a desire to continue learning and applying new knowledge. In this chapter, we'll see what makes for good facilitation, why facilitated training is preferable to most other alternatives, how participant interaction adds value to the training experience, how to facilitate online and in other nontraditional workshop settings, and how to handle sticky training situations that may crop up during the delivery of the workshops.

Facilitation: Making the Difficult Seem Easy

The *Oxford English Dictionary*'s primary definitions of "facilitate" provide a veritable checklist for what makes a truly great facilitator:

1. a. trans. To render easier the performance of (an action), the attainment of (a result); to afford facilities for, promote, help forward (an action or process).

   b. To make easier or less abstruse; to simplify. Obs. rare.

2. To lessen the labour of, assist (a person).

In fact, living up to the two portions of this definition might even be said to be the ultimate purpose of training in general. As a project management workshop facilitator, your long- and short-term objectives include:

- **Making it easier to obtain project management training.** This part of your role as project management training facilitator begins from the moment you make the commitment to deliver the training. You help make training available to the broadest possible audience by:

  - "Feeling the pain" within your organization and responding with an initial plan to deliver project management training to help address perceived knowledge gaps

  - Finding support to fund and sponsor the project management training activities

  - Selling other managers and employees on the concept that time spent in project management training will benefit them and the entire organization

  - Making training available at times and locations that allow the optimal number of employees to participate

  - Simplifying the registration and confirmation process so that learners and their managers can easily arrange to attend the workshops

  - Reminding attendees of upcoming training events to minimize no-shows.

Each of these activities makes project management training more accessible and more inviting, while at the same time removing some of the common barriers to enrollment—such as lack of line management support for the training effort and employee resistance to bureaucratic registration procedures.

◆ **Working with your organization to set and meet training goals.** Often, organizations simply know that they need *something* but have difficulty in defining exactly what they expect from project management training. In chapter 3, you examined some methods of getting to the real, most pressing project management training needs in your organization. Your ability to interact, ask probing questions, listen well, and help clarify and interpret learning requirements will facilitate the often difficult task of identifying the organization's true training requirements.

◆ **Provide physical facilities and materials so that learning can take place.** Sometimes we're so engaged in the lofty business of defining learning objectives and designing elaborate long-term curricular goals that we forget that, for learning to take place, our workshop participants will need tables, chairs, pens, instructional materials, and ready access to snacks and washroom facilities. Failure to plan for these rather mundane but essential items can turn the best-designed workshop into an episode of *Survivor.*

◆ **Accelerate the learning process by simplifying and clarifying difficult concepts.** Project management is a vast subject, and the depth of knowledge in the area continues to expand. There are numerous programs offering an M.B.A. in project management and even a few Ph.D. programs. Our one- and two-day workshops cannot pretend to compete with these programs, yet there are numerous topics in project management that must be covered to prepare our participants for managing projects. We'll need to be creative in finding ways to introduce these topics without "dumbing them down" too much. When some project management trainers have tried to cram an excessive amount of detail into a short learning experience, the results usually have been less than satisfactory. This book follows Mies van der Rohe's famous dictum that "less is more." We'll strive for simplicity and rely on a few good examples that our participants can apply in exercises to help make clear some of the key areas in project management. As facilitator, you'll want to develop your own set of analogies and explanations to help illustrate points. The more of these in your repertoire, the better job you'll be able to do in making the difficult seem easy.

◆ **Further accelerate the process by promoting team learning and hands-on practice.** Through the introduction of group learning exercises, you can effectively take advantage of the diversity of knowledge in your workshops and ensure that participants learn not just from the materials presented but—by working together on applications of project management techniques—from one another as well.

◆ **Helping learners reach closure about what they've learned through debriefing and other facilitation techniques.** By seeing to it that every major learning activity includes the sharing of discoveries and lessons learned, you help solidify new learning and set the stage for building on it in the future. By leading debriefing discussions after learning activities, supplementing exercises with short self-assessment tools, and continuing to ask "What's next?" you'll reinforce learning and help participants view their acquisition of project management knowledge as an ongoing process.

◆ **Provide performance support mechanisms after the training is over.** You further facilitate project management learning through the provision of post-workshop resources to support your project managers and team members in applying their project management training after completing the workshops. These might include "alumni newsletters" featuring project management tips and announcements about upcoming training opportunities, intranet discussion forums centered around project management issues, online tools and templates, links to project management resources, refresher presentations, and other means.

Why Facilitation Is So Important in Project Management Training

Learning to use a word-processing program, complete a purchase order, or perform other job-related tasks can occur without someone facilitating the learning. Even though the learner will apply those skills in working with others in the organization, there is no compelling need to look for common threads in previous experiences, gather consensus, or develop shared meaning from the learning activity. Project management is another matter altogether. Few other knowledge areas lend themselves more to facilitated learning experiences than the discipline of project management. The organizations most successful with project management have traditionally been those who continue to adapt and apply new learning as more and more of their employees become adept at project management practices and begin to hone good tools into even better ones. Facilitated project management training can lay a solid foundation for current and future learning, seeing to it that participants start from the beginning to think about how common repeatable practices can improve project performance and about how they can apply those practices to their current situations.

Facilitated project management workshops address such important issues as:

◆ **Why are we here?** Your first challenge may be establishing within the workshop attendees a readiness to acquire project management skills. Starting with participants sharing their project experiences provides common ground for new learning and helps point to common needs and solid reasons for learning new tools and techniques. Without adequate facilitation, participants may fail to see value in the learning objectives and to take ownership of their learning. Your job is to see to it that the participants are active learners, not passive observers.

◆ **How do we do it here?** Making project management training relevant requires a demonstration that there is commitment to the process of project management. Discussions of current practices, tools, and templates used in the organization, along with real-world examples taken from previous projects, will elevate the training experience from a theoretical exercise to a practical forum for sharing current best practices.

◆ **How does it work?** By leading your participants through a series of team exercises, you make it possible for them to explore new tools and techniques in a non-threatening environment where they are able to make mistakes and learn from them without penalty. Simulations and games require debriefing and discussions about how those activities resemble or differ from the participants' on-the-job experiences. Facilitated practice of this sort usually offers insights that individual learning activities seldom afford.

♦ **But that'll never work here!** Not all of the project experiences shared by the group are going to be glowing success stories. Don't be surprised to hear about inadequate management support, unreasonable schedules, and numerous other negative experiences. Rather than trying to avoid these issues, you as facilitator have an opportunity to make a genuine difference in your organization by openly discussing them and pointing to project management tools that can address such realities. Your workshops should always include discussions about how to use project charters, which document agreements about the project; communication tools; and risk management as a means of counteracting negative forces that inhibit success in managing projects. Facing these issues head-on can be one of the most valuable parts of a well-orchestrated project management training effort.

Addressing these four concerns throughout the training keeps it relevant to your audience and eases the transition from the training room to the workplace. When these issues are not addressed, the training loses its credibility and applicability once the workshop is over.

Collaborative Learning in Project Management Training

Managing and participating on project teams requires more than knowledge about project management and the content of the project itself. It also requires the ability to work effectively in teams, sharing ideas as well as leadership in producing project deliverables and juggling priorities of schedule, cost, and quality. A well-rounded project management training experience will include plenty of opportunity to practice collaborative techniques, so your workshops should have some components that require team interaction and cooperation.

Project post-mortems usually contain sections that evaluate how well the team functioned. You will want to point out to workshop participants that team activities are intended to simulate team efforts on real projects and you should be sure that your examples of lessons learned include questions about team effectiveness. Try to include learning objectives that address team dynamics in project management and let participants know that these will include discussions of team processes as part of the overall coverage of project management skills.

Facilitation Times Three: Three Platforms for Facilitating Project Management Workshops

In the past, there was one primary method for delivering facilitated project management training: the traditional training room, where facilitator and workshop participants interacted during the training activities. In today's world of "virtual everything," you have additional platforms for interaction with workshop participants over time and distance. In each of the three methods listed below, your role as facilitator remains much the same as it is in the training room: to act as a guide throughout the workshop and to promote participant interaction and shared understanding.

METHOD ONE: LIVE INTERACTIVE WORKSHOPS

This is the kind of facilitated training everyone has experienced. Here you have at your disposal all the traditional tools of a skilled facilitator. You can read facial expressions and body language, observe team interaction during exercises, and intervene immediately if the training appears to veer off-course. Class discussions and debriefings occur in real-time so everyone stays "on the same page" as the workshop progresses. In an ideal world, all workshops might be live interactive ones with all participants in the same room with the instructor. However, today you may need to find creative alternatives to live training, trying as much as possible to mimic the kinds of facilitation that come naturally in the training room.

METHOD TWO: REAL-TIME VIRTUAL WORKSHOPS

Virtual training has been around for a number of years in the form of video conferencing. This kind of training was once only available to organizations with access to facilities with specialized phone lines and cable connections. Today, however, virtual training platforms include Web-based conferencing. Typically these platforms allow you as facilitator to interact with audience participants who are logged into your workshop on a set day at a set time for a session ranging from half an hour to several hours in length. Your interaction with the audience usually consists of questions to and from the audience at various points within the presentation. Usually, your presentation (almost always in PowerPoint) is the focal point of the discussion as each participant sees your presentation slides shared over the Web. Questions and answers can be either in the form of spoken transmission over the audio connections for the presentation or in the form of "chat windows" where participants and facilitator enter typed questions and responses. You as facilitator can use such tools as instant polling of your audience (most platforms provide mechanisms for these), pausing frequently for Q&A, and carefully structured audience discussions using a mini-agenda on one of the slides in your presentation.

Although these kinds of online facilitated sessions may be useful for presenting introductory training or for review of previously covered topics, they tend to preclude the kind of interaction discussed earlier in this chapter. For that reason, it's important to reserve this method for short introduction or review sessions. (One of the great advantages of these sessions is the ease with which they can be recorded and played back over the Web after the initial live session has been completed. However, if you intend to record the session, you may actually want to minimize some of the interactive elements because they will often lose relevance to subsequent viewers.)

METHOD THREE: FACILITATED ASYNCHRONOUS VIRTUAL WORKSHOPS

This method of training—a specialized application of e-learning—may be the single most effective means of delivering project management training outside the traditional training room. Don't be frightened off by the rather daunting terminology. Each of the four words has significance:

◆ **Facilitated.** In much of e-learning, the primary interaction is between the learner and the online learning content. Here, however, you as facilitator continue to maintain an important role in guiding and interpreting the learning process, facilitating team discussions and activities, and orchestrating lessons learned and debriefing. You create and sustain a virtual learning community throughout the duration of the workshop.

◆ **Asynchronous.** Asynchronous training does not require participants to be online at a prescribed time or in general to interact with others in the workshop in real time. They are able to choose their own participation times. Frequently, asynchronous training means that learning can occur at any time for as long as the training is available on the online platform. In *facilitated* asynchronous training, however, training participants work in a learning community and cover the same content within a prescribed timeframe (usually a one-week period), during which team members and the facilitator interact using email and threaded discussions. In purely asynchronous workshops, chat and other real-time features are merely optional, so that participants have maximum flexibility for participation during each of the timeframes that make up the workshop agenda. Most often, team activities are accomplished using some combination of email, threaded discussions, online chat, and teleconferencing. Participants then share the results of those real-time activities with the entire group in the form of documents, PowerPoint presentations, and other workshop deliverables that can be shared on the online platform for the class.

◆ **Virtual.** Just as "asynchronous" means that participants need not be together at specific times, "virtual" means that the workshop walls extend as far as Web connections reach; that is, almost anywhere. As your audience spreads around the globe, it becomes even more important to minimize requirements for participation at specific hours of the day. Global conference calls too often require someone (and it might be you) to get up in the middle of the night to participate in the call. Try to set up your course activities in such a way that few, if any, such calls are necessary.

◆ **Workshops.** Unless there are individual and team activities that occur during the course of the training, you are not really delivering a workshop. Make sure your virtual workshops include both topical discussions, lessons learned, and activities requiring team collaboration. Be creative in coming up with additional ideas for promoting group interaction in a virtual environment.

Anticipating and Addressing Problem Situations and Problem Participants

Every facilitator would prefer to think that problem situations and problem participants will not show up in his or her workshops. Uncomfortable situations will arise no matter how carefully you plan your workshops, but there are quite a few proactive steps you can take to help anticipate and prevent some of the difficulties encountered in project management workshops.

◆ **Know your audience.** Find out as much as you can about the experience levels and expectations of your participants. Use a questionnaire to gather some of the information. Also, open most workshops (live or online) with an ice-breaker exercise that allows participants to introduce themselves and share their expectations about the workshop.

◆ **Manage expectations.** Have an agenda posted in the front of the room (in a live classroom) or in the announcements page of your on-line classroom, which spells out the topics and approximate times for workshop activities.

◆ **Clearly state learning objectives and ask the audience to rank them in importance.** Make sure the participants understand why they are there and that the objectives have relevance to as many of the audience as possible. Ask them which objectives are most important to them, but make certain they understand that you will be addressing all the objectives—unless you, your audience, and those who requested the training have agreed to cover the participants' stated objectives "by request."

◆ **Spot the "resident experts" and enlist their help.** You may wind up with a number of participants who already know (or think they know) a lot about project management. They will frequently find the materials too simple or the pace too slow for their taste, whereas the rest of the group is working and responding well to the workshop as you've designed it. The best approach here is to face the problem head-on as early as you spot it and ask them to assist in helping others in their group to master the materials. This approach may not always work, but you will at least have recognized their needs and given them an opportunity to demonstrate their expertise and apply it in helping others.

◆ **Unwilling draftees.** Try as you might, you may wind up with departments who decide to make attendance at your workshop mandatory. Sometimes salary reviews and even continued employment are predicated on staff attending a certain number of training activities. This kind of coercive policy may fill seats in the workshops, but your audience—being literally captive—will often be less than eager participants. You already have a few tips for dealing with resident experts. You then have to figure out how to build in incentives for the unwilling and clueless, who have no idea why they are attending other than the fact that they were told to—or this group will give you plenty of opportunity to exercise your best facilitation skills.

Try to help these draftees identify some reasons for acquiring project management knowledge beyond "my boss made me take this workshop." See if there are other areas where they might apply the information in the workshop, even hobbies or other outside activities. If nothing else, you will have acknowledged the situation for what it is and may gain their trust by being honest and attempting to be genuinely helpful.

What to Do Next

- ◆ Think about your audiences. Each participant has both a "good twin" and an "evil twin." The "good twin" is your model participant. Imagine a room full of these ideal individuals, pick any one of the facilitated activities found in chapters 7 through 9, and jot down the kinds of behaviors they'd exhibit. Now, imagine your worst nightmare: a room full of "evil twins." Do the same exercise and jot down how it might go. Is there anything you might do to counteract the negative behavior? Could you save the day with a group like this? You may be surprised to find that when you've finished this exercise you've identified some preventative measures for managing your most likely audience: a mixture of ideal and less-than-ideal participants.

- ◆ Do the same thing for yourself as facilitator, using what you know about your best qualities and how you perceive yourself when you're at something less than your prime. Again, most people who try this experiment manage to discover some useful insights that help them improve their facilitation skills.

- ◆ Narrow your choices. Decide which workshops you are committed to prepare and facilitate and begin working through the activities and debriefings in detail. Start to visualize the flow of activities, taking into account what you know at this point about your prospective audience. Make sure you have a clear idea of how each activity supports the stated learning objectives. Ask yourself what kinds of questions or objections your participants might raise.

- ◆ Prepare to evaluate your workshops. Read chapter 6 with the thought of how to align your facilitation plan with your evaluation criteria. "Starting with the end in mind" can help you focus your facilitation efforts on those areas that your organization has determined to be the most essential.

- ◆ E-learning readiness check (continued). If you have decided that you will be delivering one or more of your workshop offerings via e-learning, find out what platforms you have available for delivering both real-time and asynchronous facilitated workshops. If you are not familiar with these platforms, arrange for a demo or check out books, tutorials, and other resources to prepare for using them.

◆ ◆ ◆

As facilitator, you (and others who may be facilitating your workshops) will be the center of project management learning activities for the organization. You bring the workshop materials to life, help your participants find relevance and practical application for the skills taught, and lead your organization to continuous improvement of its project management training program. Without you, the texts, PowerPoint slides, and handouts have limited value. In your skilled hands, they become valuable training assets.

Chapter 6

Evaluating Your Project Management Training

What's in This Chapter?

- ◆ How to decide what to measure

- ◆ Which evaluation models have been successful

- ◆ How to adapt the sample evaluation forms in this workbook

- ◆ Some do's and don'ts in evaluating your project management training

- ◆ How to use the evaluation process for continuous improvement in your project management training effort

By now you are nearly ready to roll out your project management training. You've determined your organization's most pressing project management training needs, set training goals and objectives, and started to design workshops for meeting those goals, using the materials in this workbook as your point of departure. Finally, you have begun planning to facilitate these workshops to ensure that the materials you present have relevance and applicability for the participants enrolled in the training.

Throughout your training needs analysis, you identified absolute and relative requirements and identified measures that might effectively measure a return on the time and cost of the project management training effort. Now you need to complete your training plan by putting into place a system for evaluating its effectiveness. In this chapter, you'll look at what to measure and how to gather feedback using forms modeled after those in this workbook. You'll also identify some evaluation best practices, as well as some pitfalls to avoid in obtaining meaningful data about your project management training program. Most important, you'll view the evaluation process as a means of continually improving your organization's project management training program so that each training event builds on the successes and lessons of the previous ones.

What Should Evaluation Measure?

Most people think of training evaluation as the process of filling out a one- or two-page form at the end of a workshop and tallying the results. As a training professional, you know that there is much more to it than that; and yet we often find ourselves trapped into having our entire training initiative judged on the basis of that one document. Let's face it: If the evals aren't good, your training program may be doomed from the start. Therefore, you will want to spend some time constructing an evaluation instrument that accurately measures the things that matter. At the same time, you want to identify other measures that look more globally at the short- and long-term effects of your training effort. In other words, you would like to gather information that eventually will tell you:

- how well the workshops addressed real business needs

- how well the workshop facilitators delivered the workshop

- how much the participants enjoyed the workshop

- whether the participants actually learned the concepts presented

- whether the participants retained those concepts once they left the training room

- whether the participants actually applied the concepts when they returned to the workplace

- if the participants did apply the concepts, whether doing so resulted in any perceptible improvement in job performance

- whether, over time, there were sufficient performance improvements to demonstrate increased revenues, reduced costs, better service, or faster throughput.

Unfortunately, many project management training programs fail to evaluate beyond the first three points—despite the fact that the remaining points were usually the reason the training program was launched to begin with.

An Important Evaluation Model You Should Know

Donald L. Kirkpatrick's four levels for evaluating training programs is probably the most frequently used evaluation model. Since the model was first introduced in 1959, Kirkpatrick has continued to hone it and provided numerous case studies to point out effective methods for measuring training success from the time of the workshop through the time when the training's effect on the organization's bottom line can be judged.

Kirkpatrick's four levels are:

- **Level One: Reaction.** In Level One, the focus is on the workshop itself.

  - Was it enjoyable?

  - Were its learning objectives relevant—and clearly stated?

  - Did the facilitator address the needs of the audience?

  - Was the facilitator knowledgeable?

  - How confident is the learner that the learning objectives were met?

  - How confident is the learner that she or he will be able to apply the learning back on the job?

  - Were the surroundings pleasant?

  - Was the pace appropriate?

  - Would the learner send a colleague to this workshop?

  Obtaining answers to these questions is essential to measuring the workshop's effectiveness. The primary time to gather this feedback is during and at the very end of the workshop itself. Waiting until later will not provide as true a picture of the learner's reaction. Therefore, this data needs to be collected *from all participants* before they leave the training room (or exit the final session of the e-learning course). But, clearly, even with overwhelmingly positive responses to all of the above questions, there is no real proof that the workshop will have lasting value to the learner.

◆ **Level Two: Learning.** Level Two goes beyond the learner's *perception* of the learning and begins to measure the knowledge and skills actually transferred to the learner by asking the following:

◆ Did the training experience result in an increase in knowledge for the learner?

◆ Did the learner master new skills as a result of the training experience?

◆ Were there any changes in the learner's attitudes or beliefs as a result of the training?

Notice that each of the questions posed at Level Two are in the form of before/after pictures. In other words, Level Two evaluation will require tests before and after the workshop to obtain an accurate measurement of results. Since this is not always possible or practical, many trainers rely on quizzes, exercises, and mastery tests to demonstrate that learning has occurred. In relying solely on such measures, you are unable to prove that the learning actually resulted from the workshop.

A more serious shortfall is the fact that most of these quizzes and master tests occur within the timeframe of the training and do not take into account the issue of skill and knowledge retention. In an ideal world, you would want pre-tests, tests of learning progress, and tests administered long enough after the workshop to determine how well the learner retained the skills and knowledge acquired. The first time out with your project management training, you may settle for some mastery tools used during the workshop itself and introduce follow-up tests at a later date.

◆ **Level Three: Behavior.** Level Two can be useful in finding out what skills and knowledge your participants acquired during the workshop. Level Three takes things a step further to find out whether the participants actually apply skills and knowledge on the job by seeking to demonstrate that the workshop had practical value and resulted in changes in the way work is performed after the workshop. Level Three asks: 1) Did the participant apply the knowledge and skills acquired in the workshop on the job? 2) Have there been positive changes in the participant's attitude since the workshop?

Level One solicited the learner's evaluation of the workshop. Level Two sought to prove knowledge and skill transfer though a combination of tests and demonstrations involving some kind of interaction with the participant. Level Three seeks feedback within the organization—usually from the participant's supervisor or from the manager of the project team to which the participant belongs—to find out if the training resulted in positive change. In addition, there may be follow-up self-assessments whereby the participant can report which knowledge and skills have helped make the job easier.

◆ **Level Four: Results.** At this level, you are looking not just for proof that the participant's behavior and attitudes have changed but also for proof that these changes have benefited the organization in some way. Level Four asks: 1) Have the participant's newly acquired knowledge and skills resulted in an overall improvement in job performance? 2) Have these performance improvements translated into increased revenues; reduced costs; improved service; or other tangible, quantifiable benefits to the organization?

Level Four not only relies on feedback from the participant's supervisor but also has to take into account past performance; the stated goals of the training as defined during the training needs assessment; and perceptions of customers, other departments, the project management office, and even such indirect stakeholders as auditors and regulatory agencies. For this reason, it isn't surprising that a significantly smaller percentage of courses wind up being evaluated at Level Four. Nevertheless, Kirkpatrick's model provides a valuable framework for planning and evaluating your project management training program—whether you stop at Level One evaluations or develop a comprehensive system of evaluation. As your program grows, you can expand your use of the framework to include all four levels.

Using and Adapting the Sample Evaluation Forms Provided in this Workbook

Each of the workshops contained in this book contains sample evaluation forms for Level One and Level Two evaluations based on the material as it appears here. You will want to modify these forms to reflect any additional learning objectives and learning content added (or removed) from your final version of the workshop. Use these forms as a starting point for evaluation. The sooner you can introduce Level Three and Level Four evaluation into your project management training program, the more you will be able to demonstrate lasting value and fine-tune workshops to reflect the unique performance requirements for project managers and team members within your organization.

Evaluation Do's and Don'ts

The following list of recommendations can help you implement an evaluation process that will measure the right things and help avoid misinterpreting feedback:

- **Do evaluate each workshop session.** Make sure every workshop session has a final evaluation. For longer workshops, create a short interim feedback form so you have an ongoing gauge of student reaction and satisfaction.

- **Do use quantification measures wherever possible.** Allow participants to express the degree of satisfaction or dissatisfaction with each workshop element.

- **Do get responses from all participants.** Short of locking workshop attendees in the room and not letting them out until they provide feedback, this can be a tougher job than it might first seem. Provide plenty of reminders about the need to complete the evaluations. Consider having an additional incentive such as a completion certificate or even a trinket or other souvenir of the event to offer in exchange for completed evaluations. Make sure you have identified any attendees who need to leave before the end of the workshop and arrange to gather feedback from them too as appropriate.

- **Do measure the things that matter.** Look first to the stated objectives for the course. After that, move on to more subjective elements within the workshop.

- **Do request participants to provide explanations, comments, and recommendations.** Remember: The purpose of evaluation is to improve your training effort based on the results of the evaluation. Merely finding out that a participant "disagreed" about meeting an objective is not as useful as finding out why that person had a negative reaction.

◆ **Don't rush participants.** Handing out the evaluation forms in the last five minutes of a workshop will almost always guarantee careless or partial feedback. Even worse for you, rushing your attendees may generate hostility that may show up in their responses.

◆ **Don't ignore negative feedback.** You shouldn't be surprised if from time to time you have one or two participants who do not favorably evaluate your workshop. Read their comments carefully and see if you can find some truth in their negative comments. A pattern of negative feedback in more than a couple of evaluations is a sign that there are some elements of the workshop (or of your delivery) that need attention.

◆ **Don't just look at evaluations for a single workshop.** Each workshop is unique, with its own set of participants. You'll want to look at each event's evaluations to measure its success. Don't stop there, however. Build a database of evaluation data so you can track patterns of feedback over time. If you are running a series of offerings of the same workshop, keep the assessment data, along with details of time, location, or audience base, so you can "slice and dice" evaluation responses to spot trends and other patterns.

◆ **Don't overreact.** It's easy to let a particularly good or bad set of evaluations skew your perception of how things are going. Study each workshop's feedback carefully and dispassionately before jumping to conclusions. Continue to ask "Why might that be so?" when you see a strongly stated comment—whether it is one of approval or of disapproval.

Using the Evaluation Process for Continuous Improvement in Your Project Management Training Effort

Initially, evaluation of your training program may be a type of "proof of concept." Assuming that your program passes this first test and becomes an ongoing training component within your organization, evaluations become an excellent means for fine-tuning each training offering. The first few times you offer the training, you should expect to find a great deal of feedback that will make you want to change some of the elements in the workshops. Among the elements needing change may be the evaluation forms themselves. For that reason, try not to print up reams of evaluation forms or shelves of course materials until you have had a chance to work through this initial honing process. Thereafter, the changes required will become fewer.

Make a "pending change log" to record changes you intend to make with the next workshop revision. Having a central place to record that information—rather than leaving it spread out in evaluation forms or carrying it around in your head—will help ensure that each revision will address any previous problems. Look carefully for suggestions received on evaluations and incorporate the most valuable ones into your pending change list.

 ## What to Do Next

◆ Revisit chapters 7 through 9. This time, review the evaluations used in each of the three workshops. Note anything you think you'll need to change (including adding your company logo or other branding).

◆ Pretend you are an attendee and fill out a couple of evaluations to be sure they feel comfortable and to get some idea of the time it takes to complete the forms. (Even better, find a few "beta testers" and have them fill out the forms, asking for feedback about ease of use and the clarity of your questions.)

◆ Decide your immediate and long-term approach to evaluation. You may already have an answer in mind. If not, begin to decide how many levels of evaluation are appropriate for your initial training effort. Look back to your needs analysis to examine any stated requirements about evaluation and determine what additional work is needed before launching the training.

◆◆◆

These first six chapters serve as an extended checklist to use before presenting the workshops in the remainder of this workbook. You may decide to use the materials as they are. On the other hand, you may by now have identified areas you want to enlarge, or otherwise adapt what's available here in the book and on the CD. At the very least, the resources here should save you a great deal of time and effort—even if you decide to make extensive changes to the materials. Do what works best for you. You are the training expert for your organization and you will know the optimal combination of pre-written and custom materials to meet your project management training needs. Good luck to you!

Half-Day Session: Project Management Overview

- The design for a half-day workshop

- The purpose and objectives of the workshop

- Instructions for how to conduct the unit

- Program agenda

The purpose of the half-day session is, as its title implies, to provide an overview of what project management is. In a brief three and one-half hours, participants get a chance to work through the project management life cycle at a very high level and briefly sketch out a project charter.

Training Objectives

- Identify the key activities in the project life cycle.

- Recognize the components of a project charter and how to be appropriately scale them based on the size of a project.

- Understand the role of the "triple constraint" in project management and apply it in determining project scope.

- Keep projects on track by managing project risks and effectively using a communication plan.

- Capture valuable project lessons and use them to define and improve project management practices within your organization.

- Develop an action plan for continuing to expand your project management knowledge.

Materials

◆ Flipchart paper.

For the instructor:

◆ Learning Activity 11–4: Post-Project Review Preview

◆ Learning Activity 11–20: Creating a Personal Action Plan.

For the participants:

◆ Notepaper

◆ Post-It notes

◆ Handout 11–3: Post-Project Review Preview

◆ Handout 11–4: Quick and Dirty Project Assessment of Management Lessons

◆ Handout 11–9: Personal Action Plan

◆ Training Instrument 11–2: Workshop Evaluation Form

◆ Training Instrument 12–4: Project Charter Worksheet

◆ Training Instrument 12–7: Risk Identification Worksheet

◆ Training Instrument 12–8: Risk Priority Worksheet

◆ Training Instrument 12–10: Post-Project Review.

CD Resources

Materials for this training session appear both in this workbook and as electronic files on the CD that accompanies this book. To access the files, insert the CD and look in its "PDF Files" directory for any training instrument, handout, or learning activity mentioned in this chapter. You will find more detailed instructions and help in locating files on the CD by referring to the Appendix, "Using the Compact Disc."

Sample Agenda: Half-Day Session

8:30 a.m.   Introduce Objectives and Agenda (10 minutes)

                Display slide 7–1 as participants enter. Welcome participants and show slide 7–2, asking them to select the three objectives that are most important to them. (They will indicate their top three objectives in completing the Workshop Evaluation Form at the end of the session.) As a brief ice-breaker, ask participants to introduce themselves and share their top three objectives.

Show slide 7–3 and discuss logistics for starting and ending times, lunch breaks, and breaks during the session, using a flipchart page to record the information for reference throughout the workshop.

8:40   Defining Project Management (10 minutes)

Show slide 7–4 and move directly to slide 7–5 to introduce the definition of a project, using the PMBOK definition of "project" as the starting point. Walk participants through the chart, which analyzes the terms shown with the idea of differentiating between projects and processes (ongoing activities that have no end). Also point out that projects produce something (products or services—as well as such things as documentation or training). Show slide 7–6 and ask if someone would like to offer a definition of project management. After hearing several suggested definitions, thank the group and let them know that their definition of what project management entails will continue to grow over time.

8:50   Life Cycle (5 minutes)

Show slide 7–7 to illustrate how projects typically are organized into phases that are collectively known as the Project Life Cycle. Show slide 7–8 and point out that even though there are many different approaches to the life cycle, this is the one that will be used for this workshop. Discuss briefly the purpose of each phase and ask participants for ideas about typical activities that would take place in each. Ask why it may be useful to use a consistent approach to managing projects within an organization by using a standard life cycle. Help conclude the discussion with slide 7–9, showing that by repeating the life cycle in future projects, project teams are able to apply valuable lessons from earlier projects, much as travelers become more proficient in navigating routes based on their earlier travels along the same highways. This is why the discussion during project closure of lessons learned is so important.

8:55   Post-Project Review Preview (20 minutes)

While showing slide 7–9, introduce Learning Activity 11–4: Post-Project Review Preview (chapter 11, page 164). After the activity, reaffirm the value of the review process in continuously improving project management within the organization.

9:15   Project Selection (5 minutes)

Display slides 7–10 and 7–11 and ask participants if any have been involved in deciding whether a project should be launched. Normally, few will have had that experience, so you needn't spend a great deal of time here. However, you should indicate that normally there are more projects than resources and that, even though many of us are not involved in the selection, part of project management entails finding benefits and other good reasons to start projects.

9:20   Project Charters (15 minutes)

Display slide 7–12 to begin discussion of the project charter. Indicate the importance of this document and emphasize it as a true "charter" or "license to do business." Define the terms on the slide, including "project sponsor," asking for examples of sponsors for projects in which some of the participants may have been involved. Note the importance of the charter as a communication document. Projects are risky undertakings, and charters provide tangible proof of support from management. Show slide 7–13 and point out that project charters serve a number of other useful purposes.

Show slide 7–14 and distribute copies of Training Instrument 12–4: Project Charter Worksheet (chapter 12, page 207). Ask participants for some of the most impressive projects they can remember in recent times. (If they seem to draw a blank, start by suggesting the lunar landing project of the 1960s or the building of the Panama Canal.) Use a flipchart and gather two or three good examples of important projects in history. Refer to the worksheet and ask participants to write down what they would consider the mission of each of those projects. Share these with the entire group and indicate that, although many of their projects may not have equal inspirational nature, it is important that every project have a clearly defined mission that can be expressed in relatively few words.

9:35   Break (10 minutes)

9:45   Writing SMART Objectives (10 minutes)

Display slide 7–15 as participants return from break. Point out that the Project Charter Worksheet asks for project objectives. Cover each of the elements of a SMART objective. Ask each participant to write one objective statement for one of the important historical projects cited, using the SMART criteria. Then have them work in pairs to fine-tune their objectives. Have five or six of the participants read their refined SMART objectives.

9:55   Stating Assumptions (10 minutes)

Slide 7–16 shows two graphics: one of a mind-reading psychic (enclosed in the universal "no" symbol) and a scribe. It may be impossible to capture every assumption people may have about the project, but the project charter should capture as many important ones as is feasible. Ask participants for some false assumptions they've encountered during previous project experiences and if they can suggest some written assumptions that might have prevented the misunderstanding.

10:05   Applying the Triple Constraint (5 minutes)

The project objectives and assumptions are two of the most fundamental activities that occur during the writing of the project charter. Another important part of the charter is the statement of project constraints.

Constraints are any pre-established requirements that affect how the project is to be completed. Show slide 7–17 as you describe the most common constraints that affect projects: time, cost, and quality or scope. Satisfaction with the third constraint could be defined as meeting the stated requirements for the project, but in any case the third constraint involves the amount of effort put into the project or the number of features delivered. Some people formally refer to these three elements as "the Triple Constraint." Others prefer the informal "fast/cheap/good." A shoe repair shop owner was reminding customers of the three constraints with his sign that read "Time, Money, Quality: Pick any two."

As you display slide 7–18, explain how the Triple Constraint inevitably requires trade-offs. If one constraint changes, one or both of the other two elements must change as well. Ask for examples of such trade-offs that the participants may have experienced either in projects or in their own personal experiences.

Slide 7–19 illustrates a recommended project tool: the priority matrix. This simple form requires the project sponsor and stakeholders to agree upon the relative priorities of each of the three constraints and to indicate any specific measurement. Go over the example provided on the slide, pointing out that the priority matrix would become part of the project charter.

10:10 Project Stakeholders (10 minutes)

Show slide 7–20 to indicate that, having completed several key sections of the project charter, the project begins to move into the project definition phase. Earlier, some of the charter may have contained preliminary information, but now it would be time to get a clearer picture of scope, stakeholders, and risks threatening the project. Suggest that a project is a little like a great dramatic production, often with a cast of thousands—er, well at least dozens—of individuals with vested interest in the project. Show slide 7–21 and describe some of the key players listed. Discuss why some of these people are on the list. Make certain everyone understands how the roles listed on the slide might be stakeholders in a project. The main point is that the array of stakeholders is much broader than most people think and that it's important to identify those who need to be involved as early as possible in order to avoid misunderstanding and missed project requirements.

10:20   Project Scope (10 minutes)

There is not sufficient time in this short version of the workshop to introduce some of the powerful tools available for managing scope. Show slide 7–22 and ask for comments about the phenomenon of "scope creep." Ask how many of the participants have experienced this and the consequences to the project. Ask for suggestions on how to manage scope via a scope statement. Indicate that there are several tools available for managing scope and that these are covered in the longer versions of the workshop. For now, the most powerful concept is being specific both about what is within scope and what is outside of scope. By clearly delimiting the boundaries of the project, project teams have a much better chance of managing expectations and negotiating successful outcomes.

10:30   Managing Risk (10 minutes)

The project charter addresses several potential risks, such as unclear mission, scope creep, mistaken assumptions, and failure to agree upon project priorities. However, in addition to clear objectives, clearly written scope statements, and early identification of important stakeholders, it's important to have formal risk management process. Show slide 7–23 and discuss how risks can be identified, ranked by importance, and managed. Distribute copies of Training Instrument 12–7: Risk Identification Worksheet (chapter 12, page 211) and provide explanations of each of its sections. Go over each of the items in detail, explaining that when we ignore a risk we decide to live with it and hope for the best (not a good idea if it's a serious threat). When we eliminate a risk, we generally change our project direction to "detour" around it (for instance, we might avoid a technical risk by using a pen-and-paper solution). When we choose to manage a risk, we are making a commitment to take steps to anticipate, help prevent, and implement a contingency plan if the risk actually does take place. In other words, managing a risk costs time and effort—rather like buying insurance. We can't buy insurance for everything, so we have to carefully examine risks to decide which are the most threatening and must be managed. If we decide to manage a risk, we will take actions that would be logged to the Risk Identification Worksheet.

Show slide 7–24 and distribute copes of Training Instrument 12–8: Risk Priority Worksheet (chapter 12, page 212). The version at the top of the slide shows the risks in the order in which they were identified. The version below shows the risks ranked by priority. Emphasize that risk priorities may change as the project evolves or as circumstances outside the project change. For example, air travel risks are considerably different now than they were a few years ago.

Ask how many participants are already performing risk assessment on projects. Commend those that are and heartily endorse risk management as perhaps the most powerful tool available to the project manager.

10:40   Break (10 minutes)

10:50   Planning the Project and Planning for Communication (10 minutes)

Show slide 7–25 as participants return from break. Indicate that the topic will now turn to project planning.

Show slide 7–26. The significance of this slide is twofold:

1. It indicates the importance of brainstorming as well as formal research in creating the project plan.

2. More important, it stresses that most project planning should be collaborative.

Show slide 7–27 to introduce the concept of the Two-Floor Rule of project communications. The main premise of the rule is to keep everyone involved in the project up to date at the appropriate level of detail *and* to be ready at all times to provide information that is relevant to his or her particular role within the organization. You don't want to focus on the last file server downtime with the CEO unless that truly is the most relevant event at the moment—probably not! Your team needs plenty of project details; your sponsor needs important financial data, updates on risks, and important milestones completed and pending. In order to keep all these levels of detail straight in an already over-burdened project manager's mind, a formal communication plan is a must. Show slide 7–28 to illustrate a typical example of a communication plan. Ask why it is important to develop a communication plan early.

11:00   Tools and Budget Issues (15 minutes)

Slide 7–29 begins to address the commonly held belief that project management is all about software. Ask participants if any of them have used a tool such as Microsoft Project. If so, ask them which parts of the software were helpful and whether they used it for reporting or planning. Depending on your organization, share with the group the value of these tools in computing and tracking costs. Try not to leave the impression that software is not important, but stress that it is only one small component of the discipline of project management.

Show slide 7–30 to move to the project implementation phase of the workshop. Spend a few minutes going over a few of the "low-tech" solutions to tracking projects shown on slide 7–31. All four of these tools are easy to implement and easy for readers to understand. They are all of the "two-floor rule" variety.

The form showing accomplishments and setbacks could certainly be a standard weekly format for even the most overtaxed project team member. Ask if there are any risks in being *too* simple and whether these kinds of reports are too subjective. The Cost-to-Date Milestones and Schedule-to-Date Milestones reporting tools, on the other hand, are unblinking in their objectivity and for that reason are both highly recommended.

Finally the Top Five Risks tool is a great way to keep track of the most threatening risks and serves as a reminder to revisit and reevaluate risks previously identified.

11:15 Project Close (15 minutes)

Show slide 7–32 and indicate that the workshop has reached the final phase of the project life cycle. Distribute copies of Training Instrument 12–10: Post-Project Review (chapter 12, page 214) to illustrate its similarity to the post-project review preview used earlier in the morning. One of the important differences is on the final page, which has a place for signatures. Show slide 7–33 and point out that every project should capture lessons learned by all key participants and that a formal presentation of findings should be a major closure point for the project. Even more important is the reminder to "Celebrate Successes!" It's a project management best practice.

Display slide 7–34 as a final reminder that project management allows teams to learn new lessons with each project. This is why the concept of continuous improvement has become an important part of the project management life cycle.

11:30 Personal Action Plans (15 minutes)

Display slide 7–35 (What's Next?) to introduce Learning Activity 11–20: Creating a Personal Action Plan (chapter 11, page 198). Use slides 7–36 through 7–38 to guide the participants through the form.

11:45 Final Words: Bibliography, Lessons Learned, Evaluations, Certificates (15 minutes)

Display slide 7–39, open the floor for final questions, collect evaluations, issue certificates, and point to the bibliography on slides 7–40 through 7–42. If there is interest in any particular item, give your recommendation.

Congratulate everyone on completing the workshop and once again wish them *bon voyage* on their journey into the world of project management.

What to Do Next

◆ Depending on your audiences, you may wish to tweak the half-day workshop by incorporating additional content from the topic modules listed in chapter 10.

◆ After the first workshop, meet with participants for a mini–focus group to see what they liked and what they would like to see added or changed for future half-day workshop attendees.

Slide 7–1

Project Management Overview

A Half-Day Workshop

Slide 7–2

Workshop Objectives

- Identify the key activities in the project life cycle.
- Recognize the components of a project charter and how to appropriately scale them based on the size of a project.
- Understand the role of the "Triple Constraint" in project management and apply it in determining project scope.
- Keep projects on track by managing project risks and effectively using a communication plan.
- Capture valuable project lessons and use them to define and improve project management practices within your organization.
- Develop an action plan for continuing to expand your project management knowledge.

Slide 7–3

Workshop Agenda

- Understanding Project Management and the Project Management Life Cycle
- Initiating and Chartering the Project
- Defining the Project
- Planning and Scheduling the Project
- Implementation: Project Execution and Control
- Project Closeout and Continuous Improvement
- What's Next?
- Bibliography

Slide 7–4

1—Understanding Project Management and the Project Management Life Cycle

Slide 7–5

What Is a Project?

"A temporary endeavor undertaken to create a unique product or service."*

Term	Means That a Project
temporary	Has a beginning and end
endeavor	Involves effort, work
to create	Has an intention to produce something (project "deliverables")
unique	One of a kind, rather than a collection of identical items
product	Tangible objects, but could include things like computer software, film or stage works
service	Might include the establishment of a day-care center, for instance, but NOT its daily operations+B1.

*2000 PMBOK Guide (p. 4).

Slide 7–6

Your Turn: What Is Project Management?

- There are few if any definitive definitions.
- Project management knowledge is shared understanding of what it takes to deliver products and services effectively.
- Your definition should evolve and continuously improve with your knowledge and experience collaborating on projects.

Slide 7–7

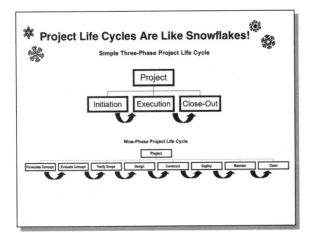

Slide 7–8

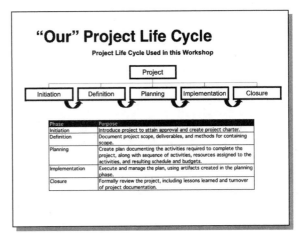

Slide 7–9

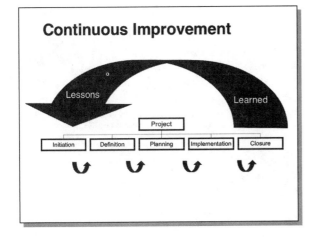

Slide 7–10

3—Selecting, Initiating, and Chartering the Project

Slide 7–11

How Projects Come to Be

- Project selection can be a difficult process, especially when there are a large number of potential projects competing for scarce dollars.
- Some selection methods are highly intuitive; others try to add rigor through more scientific selection processes.

Slide 7–12

The Project Charter

- The project charter is the project's "license to do business."
- It should come from someone outside the project itself with funding-access, resource-assignment, and decision-making authority sufficient to support the project. This person is usually referred to as the project sponsor.

Slide 7–13

Why Have a Project Charter?

- Primary purpose: To get approval to proceed with the project and obtain sufficient approval for resources to move to the next phase of the project.
- Communicate to stakeholders and other interested parties the mission and the project's objectives.
- Communicate to the project team what they are expected to accomplish.

Slide 7–14

Project Charter Components*

- Project Mission
- Project Scope
- Project Objectives
- Project Assumptions
- Project Constraints
- Milestones
- Project Risks
- Stakeholders
- Signature Page Granting Authority to Proceed

* In some organizations, the project charter is an evolving document. Many of the components listed will change as the project moves into the Project Definition Phase.

Slide 7–15

Writing SMART Objectives

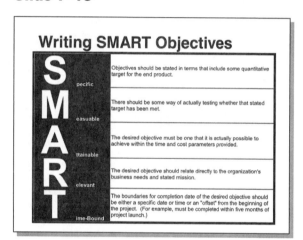

Specific	Objectives should be stated in terms that include some quantitative target for the end product.
Measuable	There should be some way of actually testing whether that stated target has been met.
Attainable	The desired objective must be one that it is actually possible to achieve within the time and cost parameters provided.
Relevant	The desired objective should relate directly to the organization's business needs and stated mission.
Time-Bound	The boundaries for completion date of the desired objective should be either a specific date or time or an "offset" from the beginning of the project. (For example, must be completed within five months of project launch.)

Slide 7–16

Project Assumptions

- Almost every lesson includes the reminder "Don't Assume!!"
- Turn that around and make it "Document Assumptions!"
  - Don't expect others to read your mind.
  - Capture as many assumptions as possible to include in your initial project charter.
  - Don't be surprised if others do not share all of your assumptions. This is the time to resolve differences—<u>before</u> the project is underway!

Slide 7–17

The Triple Constraint

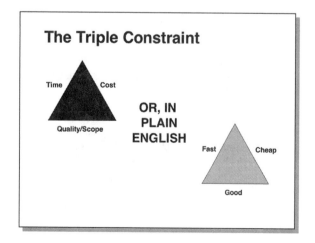

OR, IN PLAIN ENGLISH

Slide 7–18

Triple Constraint Trade-Offs

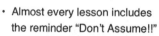
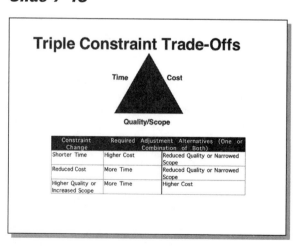

Constraint Change	Required Adjustment Alternatives (One or Combination of Both)	
Shorter Time	Higher Cost	Reduced Quality or Narrowed Scope
Reduced Cost	More Time	Reduced Quality or Narrowed Scope
Higher Quality or Increased Scope	More Time	Higher Cost

Slide 7–19

Triple Constraint: Setting Priorities

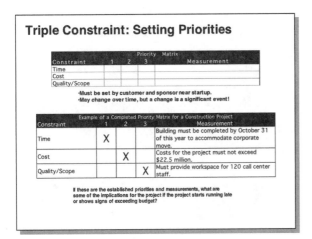

	Priority Matrix			
Constraint	1	2	3	Measurement
Time				
Cost				
Quality/Scope				

·Must be set by customer and sponsor near startup.
·May change over time, but a change is a significant event!

Example of a Completed Priority Matrix for a Construction Project				
Constraint	1	2	3	Measurement
Time	X			Building must be completed by October 31 of this year to accommodate corporate move.
Cost		X		Costs for the project must not exceed $22.5 million.
Quality/Scope			X	Must provide workspace for 120 call center staff.

If these are the established priorities and measurements, what are some of the implications for the project if the project starts running late or shows signs of exceeding budget?

Slide 7–20

3—Defining the Project

Slide 7–21

Project Stakeholders: Partial List of Candidates for Stakeholder Roles

- Project benefactor and upper management
  - Project sponsor
  - Project Office/project advisory boards
  - Executive Management
- Project requestor
- Project manager and team
  - If a team member has a line manager, he or she is a key stakeholder as well. (He or she holds the strings for your team member.)
- Internal Consultants
  - Legal
  - Audit
  - Telecommunications
  - IT infrastructure
  - Quality assurance
  - Human Resources Department
- External entities affected by the project
  - Customers
  - Vendors
  - Governmental agencies
  - Other regulatory bodies

Slide 7–22

Defining Scope

- Product Scope versus Project Scope
  - Product Scope: The sum of the features that make up the product or service created by the project.
  - Project Scope: All of the activities and resources required to produce the target product or service.

Slide 7–23

Risk Identification Worksheet

- Enter risk <u>Scenario</u> (how an event could jeopardize project outcome).
- Rate probability, impact, and degree of control using rating scale of:
  - 1 = Low
  - 2 = Medium
  - 3 = High
- Compute risk index using formula:
  $$\text{Risk Index} = \frac{\text{Probability * Impact}}{\text{Control}}$$
- If possible, enter financial impact.
- Determine actions to take:
  - Ignore (do nothing)
  - Eliminate (sidestep)
  - Manage
- For managed risks, indicate mitigations and contingencies and assign risk manager.
- Log actions taken as they occur.

Risk Identification Worksheet

Scenario:

Probability	Impact	Control	Index

Financial Impact:

Action to be Taken: ☐ Ignore   ☐ Eliminate   ☐ Manage

Mitigations:

Contingencies:

Manager of This Risk:

Actions Taken

Action:	Date:

Slide 7–24

Giving Risks Priorities

Maintain inventory of all risks identified—updating probabilities, impacts, and controls if changes occur.

Risk ID	Risk Priority Worksheet Risk Scenario	Probability	Impact	Control	Index
1	Key stakeholders unavailable during project definition phase	2	3	2	3
2	Vendors late in delivering required software for security system	2	2	1	4
3	Loss of key team member in middle of project	1	3	2	1.5
4	Power failure due to seasonal storms	1	3	1	3
5	Final regulations controlling administration of new system late	2	3	1	6
6	Scope changes require additional tasks and resources	2	3	2	3

Focus attention on the risks with the highest indices!!!

Risk ID	Risk Priority Worksheet Risk Scenario	Probability	Impact	Control	Index
5	Final regulations controlling administration of new system late	2	3	1	6
2	Vendors late in delivering required software for security system	2	2	1	4
1	Key stakeholders unavailable during project definition phase	2	3	2	3
4	Power failure due to seasonal storms	1	3	1	3
6	Scope changes require additional tasks and resources	2	3	2	3
3	Loss of key team member in middle of project*	1	3	2	1.5

* How would this change if you learned that a team member has announced that she is a finalist for a new position at the home office 1,500 miles away?

Slide 7–25

4—Planning and Scheduling the Project

Slide 7–26

Slide 7–27

Communication Made Simple

The Two-Floor Rule

– Every stakeholder should receive information at just the right level of detail for them.
– High-level managers won't want to see all the gory details of the project.

– Your team members need to see a great deal more.
– If your level of reporting is appropriate, and one of your stakeholders steps into the elevator and asks about the status of the project, you should be able to brief him or her by the time the elevator stops two floors away.

Slide 7–28

Communication Plan

Communication	Format	Frequency	Distribution
Team Briefing	Restricted Intranet	Daily at 9:00	Team and stakeholders with access to secure project info area
Weekly Web Bulletin	Internal Intranet	Weekly	Team, sponsor, senior management
Technical Incident Report	Email	Immediately after Incident	Webmaster, IT Department
Budget and Schedule Detail	Spreadsheets and Detailed Gantt Chart	Bi-Weekly	Sponsor, Senior Management
Accomplishments and Setbacks	Email and Intranet	Weekly	All internal stakeholders
Schedule Milestones	Email and Intranet	Weekly	All internal stakeholders
Cost-to-Date Milestones	Email and Intranet	Weekly	All internal stakeholders
Current Top Five Risks	Email and Intranet	Weekly	All internal stakeholders

Slide 7–29

A Word About Tools

- Many people assume that project management is about management software.
- That's like saying that residential construction is all about hammers!
- Such tools will often make your work simpler and handle complex calculations with ease.
- However, without a solid understanding of PM concepts, the tools often provide an illusion of project control that does not exist.
- Learn the concepts, then the tool.

Slide 7–30

5—Implementation: Project Execution and Control

Slide 7–31

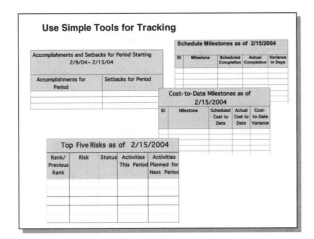

Use Simple Tools for Tracking

Slide 7–32

6—Project Close and
Continuous Improvement

Slide 7–33

Stakeholders Report/Celebration

- Communicate Results
- Pinpoint Successes
- Propose Maintenance/Corrective
  Measures if needed
  - share contributing success factors
  - present plans for corrective action
- "Sharpen the Saw" for the future
  Project Best Practices
- Celebrate Successes!!!!

Slide 7–34

Continuous Improvement

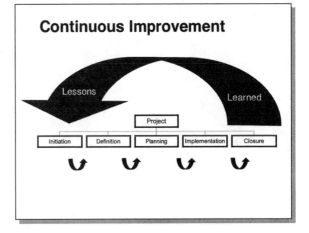

Slide 7–35

7—What's Next?

Slide 7–36

Personal Action Plan

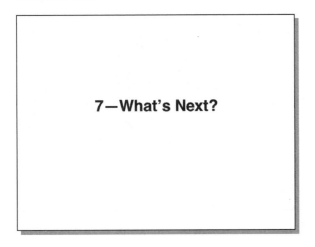

Slide 7–37

Personal Action Plan (continued)

These are the knowledge areas and skills that were not covered (or not covered in sufficient detail) but about which I would like to learn more.

These are the steps I plan to take immediately

Thse are the steps I want to take within the next 6 months

These are goals related to project management that I want to achieve within the next two years.

Slide 7–38

Personal Action Plan

- This plan is your plan and you need not share it with anyone else in the workshop.
- However, find a colleague with whom you can share your plan.
  - Make this "Project Management in the First Person" and set out to put in place the steps you listed to meet your stated goals.
- Much success in the future!!

Slide 7–39

Questions?

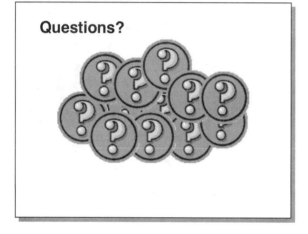

Slide 7–40

Bibliography

Slide 7–41

Bibliography

Adams, John R., and Bryan Campbell. *Roles and Responsibilities of the Project Manager* (4th edition). Upper Darby, PA: Project Management Institute. 1990.

Baker, Sunny and Kim. *The Complete Idiot's Guide to Project Management*. New York: Alpha Books, 1998.

Bennatan, E.M. *On Time Within Budget: Software Project Management Practices and Techniques* (3rd Edition). New York: Wiley, 2000.

Brooks, Fredrick. *The Mythical Man-Month*. Reading, PA: Addison-Wesley, 1995.

DeWeaver, Mary F. and Lori C. Gillespie. *Real-World Project Management: New Approaches for Adapting to Change and Uncertainty*. New York: Quality Resources, 1997.

Dinsmore, Paul C. *Human Factors in Project Management*. New York: AMACOM, 1990.

Doyle, Michael and David Straus. *How to Make Meetings Work*. New York: Jove Books, 1982.

Greer, Michael. *The Manager's Pocket Guide to Project Management*. Amherst, MA: HRD Press, 1999.

Greer, Michael. *The Project Manager's Partner: A Step-by-Step Guide to Project Management*. Amherst, MA: HRD Press, 1996.

Haynes, Marion E. *Project Management*. Menlo Park, CA: Crisp Publications, 1989.

Laufer, Alexander and Edward J. Hoffman. *Project Management Success Stories: Lessons of Project Leadership*. New York: Wiley, 2000.

Lewis, James P. *Fundamentals of Project Management*. New York: AMACOM, 1997.

Lock, Dennis. *Project Management* (6th edition). New York: Wiley, 1996.

Slide 7–42

Bibliography

Martin, Paula and Karen Tate. *Getting Started in Project Management*. New York: Wiley, 2001.

Meredith, Jack R. and Samuel J. Mantel, Jr. *Project Management: A Managerial Approach* (5th edition). New York: Wiley, 2003.

Penner, Donald. *The Project Manager's Survival Guide*. Columbus, OH: Battelle Press, 1994.

Peters, Tom, *Reinventing Work: The Project 50: Fifty Ways to Transform Every "Task" Into a Project That Matters*. New York: Alfred A. Knopf, 1999.

Project Management Institute. *A Guide to the Project Management Body of Knowledge (PMBOK Guide)* (2000 edition). Newtown Square, PA: Project Management Institute, 2001.

Roberts, W. *Leadership Secrets of Attila the Hun*. New York: Warner Books, 1987.

Schrage, Michael. *Shared Minds: The New Technologies of Collaboration*. New York: Random House, 1990.

Thomsett, R. *People and Project Management*. Englewood Cliffs, NJ: Yourdon Press, 1980.

Verzuh, Eric. *The Fast Forward MBA in Project Management: Quick Tips, Speedy Solutions, and Cutting-Edge Ideas*. New York, Wiley, 1999.

Wideman, R. Max, editor. *Project and Program Risk Management: A Guide to Managing Project Risks and Opportunities*. Newtown Square, PA: Project Management Institute, 1992.

Wysocki, Robert K., et al. *Building Effective Project Teams*. New York: Wiley, 2001.

Wysocki, Robert K., et al. *Effective Project Management*. New York: Wiley, 1995.

Full-Day Session: Project Management Jump-Start

- The design for a one-day workshop
- The purpose and objectives of the workshop
- Instructions for how to conduct the unit
- Program agenda

The full-day version of the training provides a brief but fairly extensive survey of the project management discipline. In an attempt to compress vital material into a single day's experience, many of the advantages of working with a project case study are lost. Instead, the material relies on shorter examples that prove to be reasonably good illustrations of concepts to be absorbed within the confines of a single day. This workshop might serve as ideal just-in-time training for team members about to be thrown into the melee of a new project. Their experiential learning will be on a real project, and the materials presented in this one-day workshop ought to provide some "heads-up" about the risks involved in projects. In fact, the training focuses more heavily on risk management and communication at the expense of multiple exercises in critical path and other techniques that can be covered in an e-course. The interaction time in this workshop is most important for zeroing in on some of the real-world thorny issues that arise in managing projects.

Training Objectives

- Create a working definition of the term "project management."
- Identify the distinguishing characteristics of projects versus other processes in an organization.

- Determine how each of PMI's Nine Project Management Knowledge Areas can help improve project performance.

- Recognize the components of a project charter and how to be appropriately scale them based on the size of a project.

- Understand the role of the Triple Constraint in project management and apply it in determining project scope.

- Calculate the critical path for a project and develop a strategy for keeping the project on track.

- Differentiate milestones from other project activities and use milestones to help track and manage project progress.

- Effectively manage project risks.

- Create a communication plan for reporting project progress and issues.

- Capture valuable project lessons learned and utilize them to define and improve project management practices within your organization.

- Develop an action plan for continuing to expand participants' project management knowledge.

Materials

For the instructor:

- Learning Activity 11–1: Ice-Breaker Mini-Project for One- and Two-Day Session

- Learning Activity 11–2: Defining Project Management

- Learning Activity 11–3: Using the Nine Project Management Knowledge Areas

- Learning Activity 11–4 : Post-Project Review Preview

- Learning Activity 11–7: Case Study Introduction—Beginning the Project Charter

- Learning Activity 11–8: Writing SMART Objectives

- Learning Activity 11–9: Applying the Triple Constraint

- Learning Activity 11–10: Identifying Project Stakeholders

- Learning Activity 11–18: Creating a Network Diagram and Calculating Critical Path for Case Study

- Learning Activity 11–19: Project Execution Simulation

- Learning Activity 11–20: Creating a Personal Action Plan.

For the participants:

- Handout 11–1: What is Project Management?

- Handout 11–2: How I Used the Nine Knowledge Areas

- Handout 11–3: Post-Project Review Preview

- Handout 11–4: Quick and Dirty Project Assessment of Management Lessons

- Handout 11–5: Project Case Study

- Handout 11–7: Cryptogram Cards

- Handout 11–8: Cryptogram Solutions

- Handout 11–9: Personal Action Plan

- Training Instrument 12–4: Project Charter Worksheet

- Training Instrument 12–5: Priority Matrix

- Training Instrument 12–6: Inventory of Potential Stakeholders

- Training Instrument 12–7: Risk Identification Worksheet

- Training Instrument 12–8: Risk Priority Worksheet

- Training Instrument 12–10: Post-Project Review

- Training Instrument 11–1: Scoring Grid for Team Projects

- Training Instrument 11–2: Workshop Evaluation Form.

CD Resources

Materials for this training session appear both in this workbook and as electronic files on the CD that accompanies this book. To access the files, insert the CD and look in its "PDF Files" directory for any handout, learning activity, or training instrument referred to in this chapter. You will find more detailed instructions and help in locating files on the CD by referring to the Appendix, "Using the Compact Disc."

Sample Agenda: Full-Day Session

8:30 a.m.   Welcome and Ice-Breaker for One- or Two-Day Session (20 minutes)

Display slide 8–1 as participants enter. Welcome them and indicate that you are going to start off with a short project simulation designed to introduce the class and to start looking right away at some basic project management issues.

Introduce Learning Activity 11–1: Ice-Breaker Mini-Project for One- and Two-Day Session (chapter 11, page 157). This activity asks groups to work as mini-project teams to perform an information-gathering project that will allow each team to introduce others in the room. They will have a couple of minutes to strategize their approach and estimate the amount of time it takes to complete the information-gathering project. Their success will be scored on the basis of their success in achieving the goals of the project and their overall ability to deliver the information as quickly and as close to their estimated completion times as possible.

Show participants the scoring model you'll be using, and indicate that they will have a chance to discuss the appropriateness of the model later. At the end of the project, tally scores and proceed to the introductions of the participants, making sure that every member is introduced.

8:50   Introduce Objectives and Agenda (15 minutes)

Show slides 8–2 through 8–3 and ask participants to select the four objectives that are most important to them. (They will indicate their top four objectives in completing the Workshop Evaluation Form at the end of the day.) Show Slide 8–4 and discuss logistics for the workshop start and end time, the lunch break, and breaks during the morning and afternoon session, using a flipchart page to record the information for reference throughout the day.

9:05   Defining Project Management (10 minutes)

Show slides 8–5 and 8–6 to introduce the definition of a project, using the PMBOK definition of "project" as the starting point. Walk participants through the chart that analyzes the terms used with the idea of differentiating between projects versus processes (ongoing activities that have no end). Also point out that projects produce something (products or services, as well as other things, such as documentation or training). Show Slide 8–7. Explain that now that they have a preliminary definition of "project," they will begin to create a working definition of "project management."

Introduce Learning Activity 11–2: Defining Project Management (chapter 11, page 159).

9:15   The Nine PMI Knowledge Areas (5 minutes)

This activity provides a brief exposure to the role of the Project Management Institute in helping improve the overall practice of project management. Show Slide 8–8 and explain how PMI has identified nine knowledge areas, each containing important project management issues. Indicate that full coverage of all nine areas could easily provide material for an M.B.A.! Show slide 8–9 and remind participants that even those without any previous formal project management training have probably used all of the areas in one way or another.

Show slide 8–10, and introduce Learning Activity 11–3: Using the Nine Project Management Knowledge Areas (chapter 11, page 162).

9:20   Project Management Life Cycles (10 minutes)

Show slides 8–11 and 8–12 and indicate that projects typically are organized into phases known as the Project

Life Cycle. If you already have a life cycle defined for your organization, then this discussion does not have to take up a great deal of time. Show slide 8–13 to illustrate that there are many different approaches to the Project Life Cycle and that organizations may choose one or several for managing projects. Usually the number of cycles ranges from three to five phases, but there are many exceptions. PMI does not favor any one life cycle model over any other. Show slide 8–14. (If you already have a defined life cycle, you may want to substitute a slide with it instead of the one provided here.) Discuss briefly the purpose of each phase and ask participants for ideas about typical activities that would take place in each. Ask why it may be useful to take a consistent approach to managing projects. Use slide 8–15 as a reminder that, by repeating the life cycle in new projects, project teams are able to apply valuable lessons learned from previous projects—much as travelers become more proficient in navigating familiar routes based on their past travels along the same highways. It is for this reason that the discussion of lessons learned that are part of project closure is so important.

9:30   Break (10 minutes)

9:40   Post-Project Review Preview (25 minutes)

Leave up slide 8–16 and introduce Learning Activity 11–4: Post-Project Review Preview (chapter 11, page 164). Often it's useful to suggest that teams use an approach such as this not only at the end of the project but as a way to get everyone "on the same page" at project launch, using their shared lessons learned as a foundation of best practices, mistakes to avoid, and risks to manage for the project.

10:05   Project Selection (5 minutes)

Show slide 8–17 to begin the discussion of project selection and initiation. Often project team members are not privy to the selection process, coming into projects only after they have been approved and funded. Today, more than ever, it's important to recognize that not every proposed project sees the light of day. The workshop introduces a couple of commonly used methods to serve as examples of selection.

10:10   Project Charters (15 minutes)

Use slides 8–18 and 8–19 to introduce the project charter. Emphasize that the charter is the document that gives approval to the project to proceed based on the information it contains. The charter is a communication tool that should provide the reader with a good grasp of what the project is all about. Next show slide 8–20 and briefly describe each of the bullet points. Comment that the charter is an evolving document, and certain elements are likely to be updated as the project progresses, each time with any changes approved. Slide 8–21 shows a copy of Training Instrument 12–4: Project Charter Worksheet. (If your organization has a similar template, substitute it here and adapt the following discussion points as needed.)

10:25   Introduction to the Case Study (20 minutes)

Still referring to slide 8–21, compare the completion of the charter as similar to a "scavenger hunt" requiring the project team to obtain information from a variety of sources. To illustrate the process of initiating a project charter, introduce Learning Activity 11–7: Case Study Introduction—Beginning the Project Charter (chapter 11, page 176). Prior to break time, ask participants to keep their partially completed Project Charter Worksheets, which you will help them expand upon when they return.

10:45   Break (10 minutes)

10:55   Writing SMART Objectives (15 minutes)

With slide 8–21 still displaying, welcome back the participants as they return from the break, and ask for any questions about the material so far, including the case study and the charter. At this point there may be some specific questions about the case study. The next activities will help further define the case and the project as the charter becomes more complete. Show slide 8–22. Describe SMART objectives, covering each of the five elements:

1. Objectives should be stated in terms that include some quantitative target for the end product.

2. There should be some way of actually testing whether the stated target has been met.

3. The desired objective must be one that is actually possible to achieve within the time and cost parameters provided.

4. The desired objective should relate directly to the organization's business needs and stated mission.

5. The boundaries for completion date of the desired objective should be either a specific date/time or an "offset" from the beginning of the project. (For example, must be completed within five months of project launch.)

Conduct Learning Activity 11–8: Writing SMART Objectives (chapter 11, page 178) to provide practice in applying the SMART criteria to project objectives. Ask to what extent these criteria help clarify the requirements of the project and project scope.

11:10   Stating Assumptions (10 minutes)

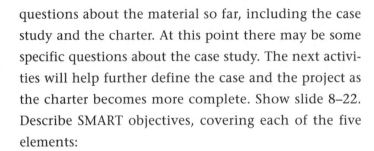

Slide 8–23 shows two graphics: one of a mind-reading psychic (enclosed in the universal "no" symbol) and a scribe. It may be impossible to capture every assumption that people may have about the project, but the project charter should capture as many important ones as is feasible. Ask participants for some assumptions from the case study they think it would be important to document. Write a few on the flipchart and ask them to come

up with at least one more for their team's Project Charter Worksheet.

11:20   Applying the Triple Constraint (5 minutes)

The project objectives and assumptions are two of the most fundamental activities that occur during the writing of the project charter. Another important part of the charter is the statement of project constraints. Constraints are any pre-established requirements that affect how the project is to be completed. Show slide 8–24 as you describe the most common constraints that affect projects: time, cost, and quality/scope. Satisfaction with the third constraint could be defined as meeting the stated requirements for the project, but in any case the third constraint involves the amount of effort put into the project or the number of features delivered. Some people formally refer to these three elements as "the Triple Constraint." Others prefer the informal "fast/cheap/good." A shoe repair shop owner was reminding customers of the three constraints with his sign that read "Time, Money, Quality: Pick any two."

As you display Slide 8–25, explain how the Triple Constraint inevitably requires trade-offs. If one constraint changes, one or both of the other two elements must change as well. Ask for examples of such trade-offs the participants may have experienced either in projects or in their own personal experiences. Slide 8–26 illustrates a recommended project artifact, called the Priority Matrix. This simple form requires the project sponsor and stakeholders to agree upon the relative priorities of each of the three constraints and to indicate any specific measurement. Go over the example provided on the slide. At this point, introduce Learning Activity 11–9: Applying the Triple Constraint (chapter 11, page 179) to provide practice in creating a Priority Matrix. Refer to the Project Charter Worksheet section on project constraints, pointing out that the Priority Matrix would become part of the project charter. Ask for any other possible constraints that might be added for the current case study.

Display slide 8–27 and point out that as the initial objectives, assumptions, and constraints become clearer, the project moves into the definition phase.

11:25   Project Stakeholders (10 minutes)

Display slide 8–28 and review the PMBOK Guide definition of the term "stakeholders." Ask for comments on each of the four points covered. How broadly can project benefactors be interpreted? (For instance, are there projects that have universal benefits, or are some targeted to just a small group of beneficiaries?) The project requestor and project team are rather obvious candidates for stakeholders, but how often are others affected by projects left out until the project is under way? Are there examples of omissions of stakeholders that have created problems later on? How do participants currently identify potential stakeholders? The checklist on slide 8–29 indicates places to look in identifying stakeholder candidates. The list should make it clearer that most projects have a more far-reaching impact than is usually thought. Getting a good handle on a project's stakeholders is a key success factor for most projects. Introduce Learning Activity 11–10: Identifying Project Stakeholders (chapter 11, page 180). At the end of the activity, remind participants that the project charter will continue to evolve and undoubtedly new stakeholders will be identified. What is most important is to get an early start so that as many key individuals as possible are kept "in the loop."

11:35   Project Scope (10 minutes)

Slide 8–30 provides brief definitions of the two main concerns of scope management for projects. Understanding and managing both of these is essential to keeping the project on time and within budget. Ask participants how they typically define scope and manage it in their current projects. What has been particularly helpful? How often has "scope creep" been a threat to project success?

11:45   Introducing a Product Context Diagram (10 minutes)

One of the powerful tools for defining scope is the Scope (or Context) Diagram. The term "context" refers to the importance of defining a product or service as the appropriate level. Display slide 8–31 to illustrate the deconstruction of the business areas of a fictitious organization called Widget World. In the example, you are trying to define a system to support sales—either as it currently exists or as it is to be after the project is completed. (One can use Product Context Diagrams for both.) The rest of the deconstruction chart represents areas outside the context of supporting sales, and direct interaction with those areas would be part the context diagram. Display slide 8–32 to illustrate a completed Product Context Diagram and point out the information flows to and from the product in relation to outside areas. Ask how some of the external areas helps define the responsibilities and boundaries of the product. Slide 8–33 shows the components of a Product Context Diagram. There are only four types of symbols used. If time allows, facilitate the creation of a Product Context Diagram for the case study.

11:55   Lunch Break (60 minutes)

12:55 p.m.   Introducing the Project Scope Diagram (10 minutes)

Welcome participants back from lunch as you display slide 8–34. Explain that this slide shows a different kind of scope diagram: that of the project itself. This diagram depicts the main project team at the center, with entities external to the project as rectangles connected to the project by arrows that represent flows to and from the central project team. The symbols used in the Project Scope Diagram are virtually identical to those used in the Product Context Diagram and are shown on slide 8–35. Just as the Product Context Diagram helps define and contain product scope, the Project Scope Diagram is a powerful tool for showing the mutual responsibilities of the project team and those outside the immediate team.

Creating a good Project Scope Diagram is one of the first steps in setting and managing expectations throughout the project. If time allows, facilitate the creation of a Project Scope Diagram for the case study.

1:05   Assessing Risk (20 minutes)

Introduce the risk assessment process by pointing out that many of the steps taken so far have helped prevent some of the "gotcha's" they identified in their Post-Project Review Preview. The tools and techniques covered so far help address project risks indirectly. Many of the steps taken so far in creating the project charter have helped address potential risks such as unclear mission, scope creep, mistaken assumptions, and failure to agree upon project priorities. It is now time to begin addressing other potential risks through a formal risk management process. All those "gotchas" from the past have shown us that the better we anticipate problems before they occur, the more likely we'll be to respond rationally and in ways that have the greatest chance of keeping our projects on track.

Show slide 8–36 to discuss how risks can be identified, ranked by priority, and managed. The slide shows Training Instrument 12–7: Risk Identification Worksheet (chapter 12, page 211) and provides explanations of each of its sections. Go over each of the items in detail, explaining that when we ignore a risk we decide to live with it and hope for the best (not a good idea if it's a serious threat); and when we eliminate a risk, we generally change our project direction to "detour" around it (for instance, we might avoid a technology risk by using a pen-and-paper solution). When we choose to manage a risk, we are making a commitment to take steps to anticipate, help prevent, and implement a contingency plan if the risk actually does take place. In other words, managing a risk costs time and effort—rather like buying insurance. We can't buy insurance for everything, so we have to carefully give priorities to risks and decide which are the most threatening and seem to warrant the time and effort required to manage.

If we decide to manage a risk, we will take actions that would be logged to the Risk Identification Worksheet. Show slide 8–37 to illustrate Training Instrument 12–8: Risk Priority Worksheet (chapter 12, page 212). The version at the top shows the risks listed in the order identified. The version below shows the risks ranked in the order of priority. We need to remember that risk priorities may change as the project evolves or as circumstances outside the project change. For example, air travel risks are considerably different now than they were a few years ago.

1:25   Project Milestones (5 minutes)

As you display slide 8–38, indicate that at this stage the project phases themselves are useful milestones, but ask if the participants can identify other useful milestones to note in the project charter. Have them add any milestones identified to the milestones section of the Project Charter Worksheet.

1:30   Work Breakdown Structure (10 minutes)

Indicate that we have now arrived at the phase of the project wherein we will create the project plan and schedule. Show slide 8–39 to introduce the concept of the Work Breakdown Structure (WBS). This is accomplished by using a technique of decomposing the project into manageable "chunks" that can be estimated, costed, and assigned to team members or outside contractors. Where do these activities come from if you've not done a project before? For right now, we'll use a "bottom up" approach to identify activities. We can brainstorm steps, gather information from our stakeholders, or consult previous project information. It's an iterative process. As organizations gain experience over time with similar projects, they generally are able to create project templates based on past projects to get a quick start on identifying activities for their current ones. Show slide

8–40 and discuss the pros and cons of templates. Caution the audience that templates are powerful tools, but that templates should never replace a thorough analysis of current project needs. The template should be a starting point, to be tailored as appropriate.

1:40   RACI Diagrams (5 minutes)

Display slide 8–41 to illustrate a high-level responsibility matrix (also known as a RACI chart). The responsibility matrix is an indispensable tool for communicating various levels of involvement in the project. Discuss the value of having these charts available to others outside of the project, such as the line manager of individuals assigned to the project. Point out how having RACI charts can help manage schedules and let others in the organization know when team members may be required for the project. Ask for one or two activities that might be required for the case study project. For each activity, have participants identify which stakeholders would be included on a RACI chart and whether they would be listed as responsible, accountable, consulted, or informed.

1:45   Planning for Communication (5 minutes)

Display slide 8–42 to introduce the concept of the Two-Floor Rule of project communications. The main premise of the rule is to keep everyone involved in the project up to date at the appropriate level of detail and to be ready at all times to provide information that is relevant to his or her particular role within the organization. You don't want to focus on the last file server downtime with the CEO unless that truly is the most relevant event at the moment—probably not! Your team needs plenty of project details; your sponsor needs important financial data, updates on risks, and important milestones completed and pending. In order to keep all these levels of detail straight in an already over-burdened project manager's mind, a formal communication plan is a must. Slide 8–43 illustrates a typical communication plan. In a larger project, each row on the plan might include a paragraph or two of details; but at the very least a grid like the one shown will be an excellent planning tool for organizing project reporting.

1:50   Break (10 minutes)

2:00   Network Diagrams and Critical Path Analysis (10 minutes)

Display slide 8–44 as participants return from break. Having completed the project charter and the Work Breakdown Structure, it is now possible to schedule the project. Indicate that scheduling normally starts by creating a network diagram. Point out that there are two kinds used in developing schedules, the AOA and AON. To illustrate each type of network diagram, show slides 8–45 and 8–46. These two diagrams depict the same network of activities. (By the way, the Gantt chart logo on the bottom of each slide is actually a mapping of the same set of tasks and dependencies.) Point out the definition of critical path on both slides and walk participants through the calculation, making sure everyone follows the logic of why the path is "critical" to the timely completion of the project. Also make sure they understand where "slack" exists on the noncritical path.

2:10   Task Sequencing, Network Diagrams, and Critical Path (25 minutes)

Display slide 8–47 and announce that the first attempt at creating a network diagram and critical path will be for a party to be held at the end of the day. (Note that this is a fictitious party, unless you decide to bring in food and beverages later!) Conduct Learning Activity 11–18: Creating a Network Diagram and Calculating Critical Path for Case Study (chapter 11, page 192). Use slides 8–48 through 8–50 to debrief.

Following the activity, display slide 8–51 and let the participants know that the diagrams included on the preceding slides were created using a project management software tool (Microsoft Project). Reassure them that in real life they might not have to perform all the calculations used in the exercise but that it is highly recommended to have a good grasp of what the software was doing. Far too often, project teams find themselves working with figures whose source they no control over. Project management software is a tool, nothing more.

2:35   Tools and Budget Issues (10 minutes)

Display slide 8–52 and announce that this is the point at which the project moves into the implementation phase. A moment ago, we had mentioned that software tools were useful in assisting with scheduling and managing project. However, it is often possible to achieve equally good results through the use of a few "low-tech" solutions for project tracking. Such solutions are both easy to implement and easy to understand by those to whom you report progress. They are all of the Two-Floor Rule variety. Show slide 8–53, which illustrates four of the simplest:

1. Accomplishments and Setbacks. This could certainly be a standard weekly format for even the most overtaxed project team member. Ask what advantages there would be in using such a simple reporting tool for team member and project reporting. Are there any risks in being too simple? What might slip through the cracks?

2. Schedule Milestones. This is a slightly more rigorous reporting tool. Because it is based on comparisons to the original plan, it works quite literally as a tracking tool for projects. It is unblinking in its objectivity and for that reason is highly recommended.

3. Cost-to-Date Milestones. This is the budgetary counterpart of the schedule milestone chart and has similar virtues. There are more sophisticated indicators available such as Earned Value calculations, but, at a minimum, this form can be incredibly useful.

4. Top Five Risks. This shows the current ranking as of the reporting date. Recall that earlier in discussing risks that risks needed reevaluation frequently. Having a regularly scheduled report such as this one can serve as a reminder to revisit and reevaluate identified risks. Point out that in so doing, it was naturally recommended that any new risks be added as well.

Slide 8–54 is another important reminder to stay on top of project scope and priorities of time, cost, and quality. If any of these change, it is almost always a sign of a major shift of project direction and may point to re-estimation of project plans.

2:45   Break (10 minutes)

2:55   Project Execution Simulation (30 minutes)

As participants return from break, display slide 8–55 to preview the transition to project close. However, announce that there is one additional activity that will give everyone another chance to plan and execute a project. The same scoring rules will apply as in the ice-breaker activity. Proceed directly to Learning Activity 11–19: Project Execution Simulation (chapter 11, page 194). (If time allows, you may also expand Learning Activity 11–19 to a 45-minute exercise that also simulates multitasking.)

3:25   Project Closeout (10 minutes)

With slide 8–55 still displayed, tell participants that what they are about to see will look very familiar. Show slide 8–56, revealing the first page of Training Instrument 12–10: Post-Project Review. Remind participants that they built their learning during the day on some of the lessons they learned in Learning Activity 11–4: Post-Project Review Preview. Briefly walk through slides 8–56 through 8–59, pointing out the few differences between this and Handout 11–3 (the preview form). Most notable is the final page, with a place for signatures. Ideally, projects should capture lessons learned by all key participants, and a formal presentation of findings should be a major closure point for the project.

Display slide 8–60 and remind participants that project reviews and project close should always be cause for celebration. Move to slide 8–61 to once again remind everyone that each project provides lessons to make the next projects run more smoothly and have a greater opportunity to succeed as project teams become increasingly adept at project management.

3:35   Personal Action Plans (15 minutes)

Display slide 8–62. Point out that at this point we are about to end the class, but this is just the beginning of what is hoped to be an exciting journey into the mastery of project management skills. This intensive one-day workshop has tried to build onto the participants' previous experiences and allow everyone to share ideas, new tools, and techniques. Each person may have his or her own answer to the question "What's Next?" Display slides 8–63 and 8–64 and begin Learning Activity 11–20: Creating a Personal Action Plan (chapter 11, page 198). Conclude with the display of slide 8–65 before moving to the final activity of the day.

3:50   Final Words—Bibliography, Evaluations, Certificates (10 minutes)

Display slide 8–66 and open the floor for final questions, collect evaluations, issue certificates, and point to the bibliography in the back of the materials. If there is interest in any particular item, give your recommendation.

Congratulate everyone on completing the workshop and once again wish them *bon voyage* on their journey into the world of project management.

What to Do Next

This workshop is the "middle ground" between a short overview like the one covered in chapter 7 and a more comprehensive two-day experience like the one outlined in the following chapter. Based on your organization's needs, you may decide to expand certain topics in the one-day version and truncate others to provide the extra time required for the expanded material. Where expansion is required, check the topic modules listed in chapter 10 for additional resources. Chapter 7 may provide you with ideas for covering a topic more quickly if you want to shorten the schedule for your new material.

After the first workshop meet with participants for a mini–focus group to see what they liked and what they would like to see added or changed for future one-day workshop attendees.

Slide 8–1

Project Management Jump-Start

A One-Day Workshop

Slide 8–2

Workshop Objectives

- Create a working definition of the term "project management."
- Identify the distinguishing characteristics of projects versus other processes in an organization.
- Determine how each of PMI's Nine Project Management Knowledge Areas can help improve project performance.
- Recognize the components of a Project Charter and how to appropriately scale them based on the size of a project.
- Understand the role of the "triple constraint" in project management and apply it in determining project scope.
- Calculate the critical path for a project and develop a strategy for keeping the project on track.

Slide 8–3

Workshop Objectives (continued)

- Differentiate milestones from other project activities and use milestones to help track and manage project progress.
- Effectively manage project risks.
- Create a communication plan for reporting project progress and issues.
- Capture valuable project lessons and use them to define and improve project management practices within your organization.
- Develop an action plan for continuing to expand your project management knowledge.

Slide 8–4

Workshop Agenda

- Introduction: What is Project Management?
- The Project Management Cycle
- Selecting, Initiating, and Chartering the Project
- Defining the Project
- Planning and Scheduling the Project
- Implementation: Project Execution and Control
- Project Closeout and Continuous Improvement
- What's Next?
  Bibliography

Slide 8–5

**1—Introduction:
What Is Project Management?**

Slide 8–6

What Is a Project?

"A temporary endeavor undertaken to create a unique product or service."*

Term	Means That a Project
temporary	Has a beginning and end
endeavor	Involves effort, work
to create	Has an intention to produce something (project "deliverables")
unique	One of a kind, rather than a collection of identical items
product	Tangible objects, but could include things like computer software, film or stage works
service	Might include the establishment of a day-care center, for instance, but NOT its daily operations.

*2000 PMBOK Guide (p. 4).

Slide 8–7

Your Turn: What Is Project Management?

- There are few if any definitive definitions.
- Project management knowledge is shared understanding of what it takes to deliver products and services effectively.
- Your definition should evolve and continuously improve with your knowledge and experience collaborating on projects.

Slide 8–8

PMI's Nine Project Management Knowledge Areas

- Integration Management
- Scope Management
- Time Management
- Cost Management
- Quality Management
- Human Resource Management
- Communications Management
- Risk Management
- Procurement Management

Slide 8–9

Where to Begin?

Look back over your previous project experiences.

Chances are, you've used a little of each of these nine areas already.

The PMBOK merely codifies them and attempts to give us a framework for understanding and applying project management knowledge productively.

Slide 8–10

Your Turn: What We Know Already

- Look back over your previous experience in project management
- How many of the nine knowledge areas did you use? (Probably all nine!)
- Take a quick inventory and point to your most successful application use of that knowledge area.
- Pick up at least one new tip from others right now!

Slide 8–11

2—The Project Management Cycle

Slide 8–12

The Project Life Cycle

General Form of a Project Life Cycle

Slide 8–13

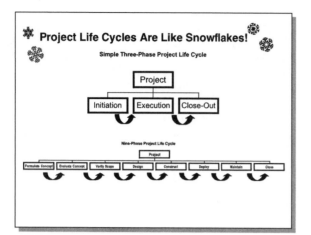

Slide 8–14

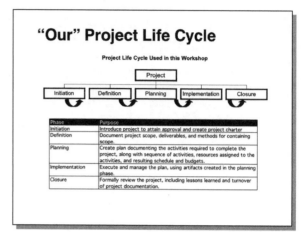

Slide 8–15

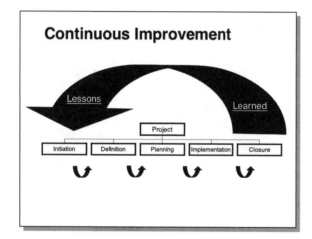

Slide 8–16

3—Selecting, Initiating, and Chartering the Project

Slide 8–17

How Projects Come to Be

- Project selection can be a difficult process, especially when there are a large number of potential projects competing for scarce dollars.
- Some selection methods are highly intuitive; others try to add rigor through more scientific selection processes.

Slide 8–18

The Project Charter

- The project charter is the project's "license to do business."
- It should come from someone outside the project itself with funding-access, resource-assignment, and decision-making authority sufficient to support the project, who is usually known as the project sponsor.

Slide 8–19

Why Have a Project Charter?

- Primary purpose: To get approval to proceed with the project and obtain sufficient approval for resources to move to the next phase of the project.
- Communicate to stakeholders and other interested parties the project's mission and the project's objectives.
- Communicate to the project team what they are expected to accomplish.

Slide 8–20

Project Charter Components*

- Project Mission
- Project Scope
- Project Objectives
- Project Assumptions
- Project Constraints
- Milestones
- Project Risks
- Stakeholders
- Signature Page Granting Authority to Proceed

* In some organizations, the project charter is an evolving document. Many of the components listed will change as the project moves into the Project Definition Phase.

Slide 8–21

Your Turn: Starting the Charter

Project Charter Worksheet

Project Mission
Write Project Mission Statement Here:

Project Scope
Brief statement of project scope. (Supplement with Product Scope and Project Scope Diagrams as part of the Appendix.)

Project Objectives
List at least three SMART Objectives.

Project Assumptions
List at least three Project Assumptions.

Project Constraints
See Project Priority Matrix in Appendix. List any other constraints here.

Project Phases
Indicate the phases of the proposed project.

Milestones
List major milestones for project identified so far. (Include at least five throughout the life of the project).

Project Risks
Attach Risk Identification Worksheets and Risk Priority worksheet.

Stakeholders
Attach Potential Stakeholders Worksheet.

Signature Page Granting Authority to Proceed
Obtain signatures of Project Sponsor and Project Manager.
Project Sponsor Signature:
Project Manager Signature:

Slide 8–22

Writing SMART Objectives

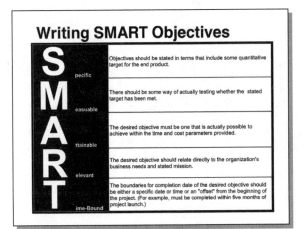

Specific	Objectives should be stated in terms that include some quantitative target for the end product.
Measurable	There should be some way of actually testing whether the stated target has been met.
Attainable	The desired objective must be one that is actually possible to achieve within the time and cost parameters provided.
Relevant	The desired objective should relate directly to the organization's business needs and stated mission.
Time-Bound	The boundaries for completion date of the desired objective should be either a specific date or time or an "offset" from the beginning of the project. (For example, must be completed within five months of project launch.)

Slide 8–23

Project Assumptions

- Almost every lesson includes the reminder "Don't Assume!!"
- Turn that around and make it "Document Assumptions!"
  - Don't expect others to read your mind.
  - Capture as many assumptions as possible to include in your initial project charter
  - Don't be surprised if others do not share all of your assumptions. This is the time to resolve differences—<u>before</u> the project is underway!

Slide 8–24

The Triple Constraint

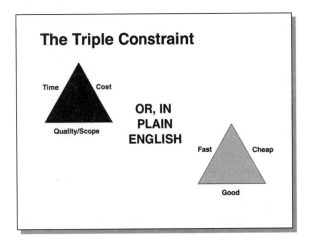

Time   Cost

Quality/Scope

OR, IN PLAIN ENGLISH

Fast   Cheap

Good

Slide 8–25

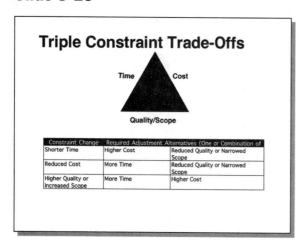

Slide 8–26

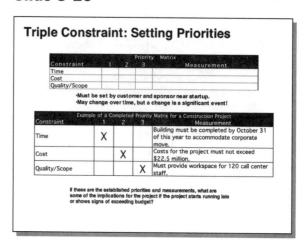

Slide 8–27

4—Defining the Project

Slide 8–28

Project Stakeholders

- "Individuals and organizations that are actively involved in the project, or whose interest may be positively or negatively affected as a result of project execution or project completion." 2000 PMBOK Guide
- Short list
  - Project benefactor
  - Project requestor
  - Project manager and team
  - Those affected by the project

Slide 8–29

Project Stakeholders: Partial List of Candidates for Stakeholder Roles

- Project benefactor and upper management
  - Project sponsor
  - Project Office/project advisory boards
  - Executive management
- Project requestor
- Project manager and team
  - If a team member has a line manager, he or she is a key stakeholder. (He or she holds the strings for your team members.)
- Internal consultants
  - Legal
  - Audit
  - Telecommunications
  - IT infrastructure
  - Quality assurance
  - Human Resources Department
- External entities affected by the project
  - Customers
  - Vendors
  - Governmental agencies
  - Other regulatory bodies

Slide 8–30

Defining Scope

- Product Scope versus Project Scope
  - Product Scope: The sum of the features that make up the product or service created by the project.
  - Project Scope: All of the activities and resources required to produce the target product or service.

Slide 8–31

Preliminary Context Diagrams : Deconstruction

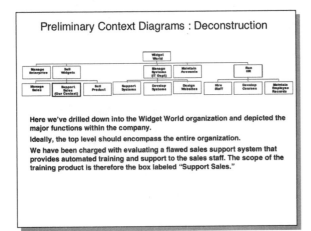

Here we've drilled down into the Widget World organization and depicted the major functions within the company.

Ideally, the top level should encompass the entire organization.

We have been charged with evaluating a flawed sales support system that provides automated training and support to the sales staff. The scope of the training product is therefore the box labeled "Support Sales."

Slide 8–32

Scope (Context) diagrams
Defining the End Product

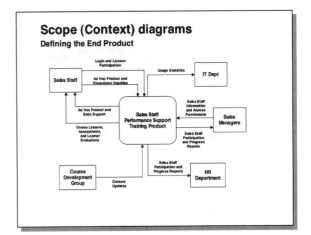

Slide 8–33

Scope (Context) Diagrams
Defining the End Product (continued)

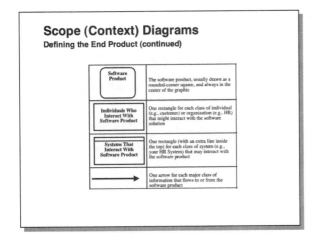

Slide 8–34

Scope (Context) Diagrams
(applied to project team charged with delivery of the product)

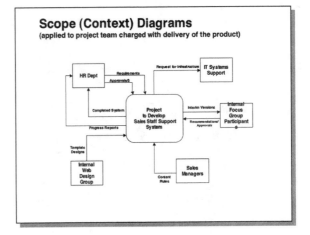

Slide 8–35

Scope (Context) Diagram
(applied to project team charged with delivery of the product - continued)

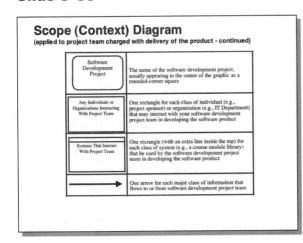

Slide 8–36

Risk Identification Worksheet

- Enter risk Scenario (how an event could jeopardize project outcome).
- Rate probability, impact, and degree of control using rating scale of:
  - 1 = Low
  - 2 = Medium
  - 3 = High
- Compute risk index using formula:
  $$\text{Risk Index} = \frac{\text{Probability} \times \text{Impact}}{\text{Control}}$$
- If possible, enter financial impact
- Determine actions to take:
  - Ignore (do nothing)
  - Eliminate (sidestep)
  - Manage
- For managed risks, indicate mitigations and contingencies and assign risk manager.
- Log actions taken as they occur.

Slide 8–37

Giving Risks Priorities

Maintain inventory of all risks identified—updating probabilities, impacts, and controls if changes occur.

Risk Priority Worksheet

Risk ID	Risk Scenario	Probability	Impact	Control	Index
1	Key stakeholders unavailable during project definition phase	2	3	2	3
2	Vendors late in delivering required software for security system	2	2	1	4
3	Loss of key team member in middle of project	1	3	2	1.5
4	Power failure due to seasonal storms	1	3	1	3
5	Final regulations controlling administration of new system late	2	3	1	6
6	Scope changes require additional tasks and resources	2	3	2	3

Focus attention on the risks with the highest indices!!!

Risk Priority Worksheet

Risk ID	Risk Scenario	Probability	Impact	Control	Index
5	Final regulations controlling administration of new system late	2	3	1	6
2	Vendors late in delivering required software for security system	2	2	1	4
1	Key stakeholders unavailable during project definition phase	2	3	2	3
4	Power failure due to seasonal storms	1	3	1	3
6	Scope changes require additional tasks and resources	2	3	2	3
3	Loss of key team member in middle of project*	1	3	2	1.5

* How would this change if you learned that a team member has announced that she is a finalist for a new position at the home office 1,500 miles away?

Slide 8–38

5—Planning and Scheduling the Project

Slide 8–39

Sources of Project Activities: Brainstorming

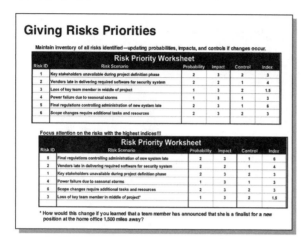

Slide 8–40

More Sources of Project Activities: Templates

- Don't reinvent the wheel!
  - As you get more projects under your belt, work with other project teams to develop templates to use as a starting point.
  - Remember, no two projects are ever exactly alike (remember the "unique" in the definition of a project). The template should be a starting point—to be tailored to the specific needs of the current project.
  - Even with the time spent in tailoring, templates can be enormous time-savers.

Slide 8–41

Assigning Responsibilities: Responsibility Matrix (also known as RACI Chart)

- Cross-reference of tasks and resources assigned to the project.

Project Item	Sponsor	Project Manager	Project Team	Project Office
Project Definition	A	A	R	I
Risk Management	A	R	R	C
Detailed Design	A	R	R	C
Weekly Web Bulletin	I	R	R	I
etc.				

R =	Responsible
A =	Accountable
C =	Consulted
I =	Informed

Slide 8–42

Communication Made Simple

The Two-Floor Rule

- Every stakeholder should receive information at just the right level of detail for him or her.
- High-level managers won't want to see all the gory details of the project.
- Your team members need to see a great deal more.
- If your level of reporting is appropriate, and one of your stakeholders steps into the elevator and asks about the status of the project, you should be able to brief him or her by the time the elevator stops two floors away.

Slide 8–43

Communication Plan

Communication	Format	Frequency	Distribution
Team Briefing	Restricted Intranet	Daily at 9:00	Team and stakeholders with access to secure project info area
Weekly Web Bulletin	Internal Intranet	Weekly	Team, sponsor, senior management
Technical Incident Report	Email	Immediately after Incident	Webmaster, IT Department
Budget and Schedule Detail	Spreadsheets and Detailed Gantt Chart	Bi-Weekly	Sponsor, Senior Management
Accomplishments and Setbacks	Email and Intranet	Weekly	All internal stakeholders
Schedule Milestones	Email and Intranet	Weekly	All internal stakeholders
Cost-to-Date Milestones	Email and Intranet	Weekly	All internal stakeholders
Current Top Five Risks	Email and Intranet	Weekly	All internal stakeholders

Slide 8–44

Network Diagrams and Critical Path Analysis

Once you've determined the activities for the project and estimated their durations, network diagrams are the next step for creating the project schedule.

Two Types:

Activity on Arrow (AOA)—nodes on the diagram connect arrows and represent activities

Activity on Node (AON)—nodes represent activities that are connected by arrows showing the precedence of activities

Slide 8–45

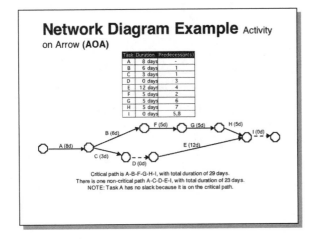

Network Diagram Example Activity on Arrow (AOA)

Task	Duration	Predecessor(s)
A	8 days	-
B	6 days	1
C	3 days	1
D	0 days	3
E	12 days	4
F	5 days	2
G	5 days	6
H	5 days	7
I	0 days	5,8

Critical path is A-B-F-G-H-I, with total duration of 29 days.
There is one non-critical path A-C-D-E-I, with total duration of 23 days.
NOTE: Task A has no slack because it is on the critical path.

Slide 8–46

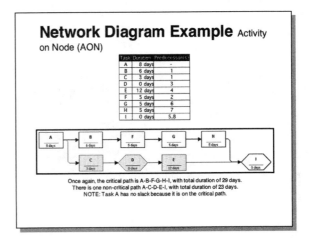

Network Diagram Example Activity on Node (AON)

Task	Duration	Predecessor(s)
A	8 days	-
B	6 days	1
C	3 days	1
D	0 days	3
E	12 days	4
F	5 days	2
G	5 days	6
H	5 days	7
I	0 days	5,8

Once again, the critical path is A-B-F-G-H-I, with total duration of 29 days.
There is one non-critical path A-C-D-E-I, with total duration of 23 days.
NOTE: Task A has no slack because it is on the critical path.

Slide 8–47

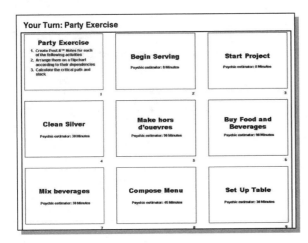

Your Turn: Party Exercise

Party Exercise
1. Create Post-It™ Notes for each of the following activities
2. Arrange them on a flipchart according to their dependencies
3. Calculate the critical path and slack

Begin Serving
Psychic estimator: 0 Minutes

Start Project
Psychic estimator: 0 Minutes

Clean Silver
Psychic estimator: 30 Minutes

Make hors d'ouevres
Psychic estimator: 90 Minutes

Buy Food and Beverages
Psychic estimator: 90 Minutes

Mix beverages
Psychic estimator: 30 Minutes

Compose Menu
Psychic estimator: 45 Minutes

Set Up Table
Psychic estimator: 30 Minutes

Slide 8–48

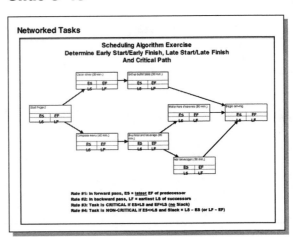

Networked Tasks

Scheduling Algorithm Exercise
Determine Early Start/Early Finish, Late Start/Late Finish And Critical Path

Rule #1: In forward pass, ES = latest EF of predecessor
Rule #2: In backward pass, LF = earliest LS of successors
Rule #3: Task is CRITICAL if ES=LS and EF=LS (no Slack)
Rule #4: Task is NON-CRITICAL if ES<>LS and Slack = LS – ES (or LF – EF)

Slide 8-49

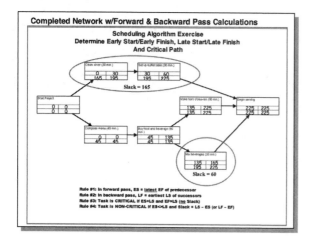

Slide 8-50

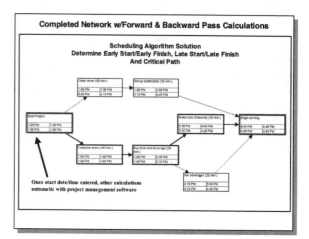

Slide 8-51

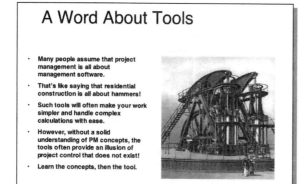

A Word About Tools

- Many people assume that project management is all about management software.
- That's like saying that residential construction is all about hammers!
- Such tools will often make your work simpler and handle complex calculations with ease.
- However, without a solid understanding of PM concepts, the tools often provide an illusion of project control that does not exist!
- Learn the concepts, then the tool.

Slide 8-52

6—Implementation: Project Execution and Control

Slide 8-53

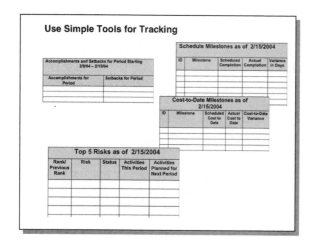

Use Simple Tools for Tracking

Slide 8-54

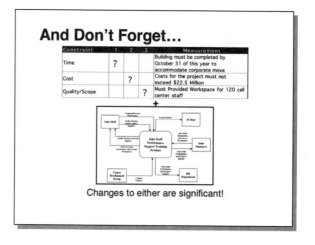

And Don't Forget...

Changes to either are significant!

Slide 8–55

7—Project Close and
Continuous Improvement

Slide 8–56

You've Already Seen the Value of This

Slide 8–57

Post-Project Review (continued)

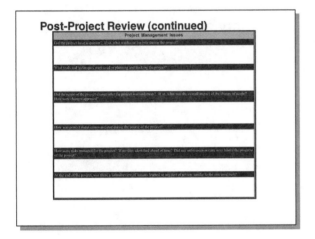

Slide 8–58

Post-Project Review (continued)

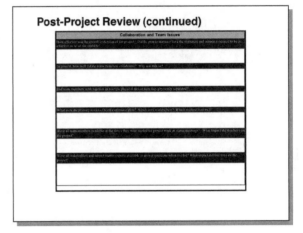

Slide 8–59

Post-Project Review (continued)

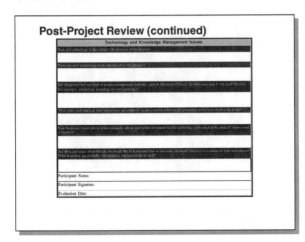

Slide 8–60

Stakeholders Report/Celebration

- Communicate results
- Pinpoint successes
- Propose maintenance/corrective measures if needed
  - share contributing success factors
  - present plans for corrective action
- "Sharpen the Saw" for future project best practices
- Celebrate successes!!!!

Slide 8–61

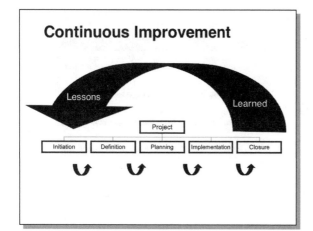

Slide 8–62

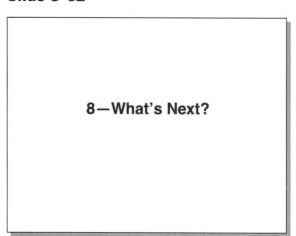

Slide 8–63

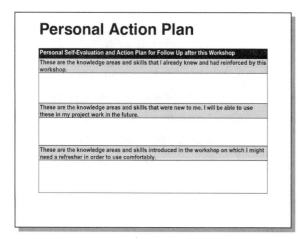

Slide 8–64

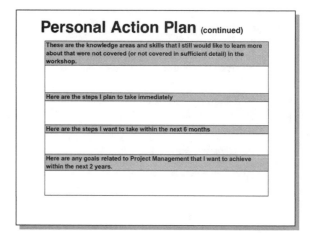

Slide 8–65

Personal Action Plan

- This plan is your plan and you need not share it with anyone else in the workshop.
- However, find a colleague with whom you can share your plan.
  - Make this "Project Management in the First Person" and set out to put in place the steps you listed to meet your stated goals.
- Much success in the future!!

Slide 8–66

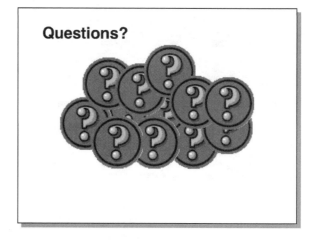

Slide 8–67

Bibliography

Slide 8–68

Bibliography

Adams, John R., and Bryan Campbell. *Roles and Responsibilities of the Project Manager* (4th edition). Upper Darby, PA: Project Management Institute, 1990.

Baker, Sunny and Kim. *The Complete Idiot's Guide to Project Management*. New York: Alpha Books, 1998.

Bennatan, E.M. *On Time Within Budget: Software Project Management Practices and Techniques* (3rd Edition). New York: Wiley, 2000.

Brooks, Fredrick. *The Mythical Man-Month*. Reading, PA: Addison-Wesley, 1995.

DeWeaver, Mary F. and Lori C. Gillespie. *Real-World Project Management: New Approaches for Adapting to Change and Uncertainty*. New York: Quality Resources, 1997.

Dinsmore, Paul C. *Human Factors in Project Management*. New York: AMACOM, 1990.

Doyle, Michael and David Straus. *How to Make Meetings Work*. New York: Jove Books, 1982.

Greer, Michael. *The Manager's Pocket Guide to Project Management*. Amherst, MA: HRD Press, 1999.

Greer, Michael. *The Project Manager's Partner: A Step-by-Step Guide to Project Management*. Amherst, MA: HRD Press, 1996.

Haynes, Marion E. *Project Management*. Menlo Park, CA: Crisp Publications, 1989.

Laufer, Alexander and Edward J. Hoffman. *Project Management Success Stories: Lessons of Project Leadership*. New York: Wiley, 2000.

Lewis, James P. *Fundamentals of Project Management*. New York: AMACOM, 1997.

Lock, Dennis. *Project Management* (6th edition). New York: Wiley, 1996.

Slide 8–69

Bibliography

Martin, Paula and Karen Tate. *Getting Started in Project Management*. New York: Wiley, 2001.

Meredith, Jack R. and Samuel J. Mantel, Jr. *Project Management: A Managerial Approach* (5th edition). New York: Wiley, 2003.

Penner, Donald. *The Project Manager's Survival Guide*. Columbus, OH: Battelle Press, 1994.

Peters, Tom, *Reinventing Work: The Project 50: Fifty Ways to Transform Every "Task" Into a Project That Matters*. New York: Alfred A. Knopf, 1999.

Project Management Institute. *A Guide to the Project Management Body of Knowledge (PMBOK Guide)* (2000 edition). Newtown Square, PA: Project Management Institute, 2001.

Roberts, W. *Leadership Secrets of Attila the Hun*. New York: Warner Books, 1987.

Schrage, Michael. *Shared Minds: The New Technologies of Collaboration*. New York: Random House, 1990.

Thomsett, R. *People and Project Management*. Englewood Cliffs, NJ: Yourdon Press, 1980.

Verzuh, Eric. *The Fast Forward MBA in Project Management: Quick Tips, Speedy Solutions, and Cutting-Edge Ideas*. New York, Wiley, 1999.

Wideman, R. Max, editor. *Project and Program Risk Management: A Guide to Managing Project Risks and Opportunities*. Newtown Square, PA: Project Management Institute, 1992.

Wysocki, Robert K., et al. *Building Effective Project Teams*. New York: Wiley, 2001.

Wysocki, Robert K., et al. *Effective Project Management*. New York: Wiley, 1995.

Two-Day Session: Project Management Essentials

♦ The design for a two-day workshop

♦ The purpose and objectives of the workshop

♦ Instructions for how to conduct the unit

♦ Program agenda

As the workshop title implies, Project Management Essentials introduces most of the fundamental concepts of project management. By providing considerably more practice and interactive time, the two-day schedule lays a foundation for further study and at the same time gives participants most of the tools and techniques needed to work effectively on a project team and create project tools with confidence.

The material in the two-day version of the workshop goes into greater depth and allows more time for practice and discussion of the concepts. Participants from the half-day and one-day versions of the class would encounter many familiar concepts but also would find sufficiently new materials here to hold their interests—especially if they attended the shorter workshops more than a few weeks earlier.

Training Objectives

♦ Create a working definition of the term "project management."

♦ Identify the distinguishing characteristics of projects versus other processes in an organization.

- Employ commonly used techniques for selecting projects from a list of candidate projects.

- Determine how each of PMI's Nine Project Management Knowledge Areas can be used to improve project performance.

- Name the key stakeholders in a project and determine ways of keeping them "on task" during the phases of a project.

- Break a project into logical phases and specify the primary activities that occur in each phase.

- Effectively use the components of a project charter and appropriately scale each of them based on the size of a project.

- Write SMART project objectives that will help define project scope.

- Document and clearly communicate project assumptions.

- Develop a procedure for managing changes in the project once it is under way.

- Create a Work Breakdown Structure (WBS) for a project.

- Sequence activities within a project based on mandatory and discretionary dependencies.

- Estimate activity durations and make appropriate adjustments as needed.

- Understand the role of "the Triple Constraint" in project management and apply it in determining project scope.

- Calculate the critical path for a project and develop a strategy for keeping the project on track.

- Differentiate milestones from other project activities and use milestones to help track and manage project progress.

- Identify, quantify, and give priorities to risks in managing a project.

- Create a communication plan for reporting project progress and issues.

- Use tools for measuring project progress in terms of time, costs, and deliverables.

- Develop a strategy for managing project resources by using a responsibility matrix for assigning project activities to resources.

- Capture valuable project lessons learned and use them to define and improve project management practices within your organization.

- Develop an action plan for continuing to expand your project management knowledge.

Materials

For the instructor:

- ◆ Learning Activity 11–1: Ice-Breaker Mini-Project for One- and Two-Day Sessions

- ◆ Learning Activity 11–2: Defining Project Management

- ◆ Learning Activity 11–3: Using the Nine Project Management Knowledge Areas

- ◆ Learning Activity 11–4: Post-Project Review Preview

- ◆ Learning Activity 11–5: Weighted and Unweighted Selection Criteria

- ◆ Learning Activity 11–6: Using Forced-Pair Comparisons

- ◆ Learning Activity 11–7: Case Study Introduction—Beginning the Project Charter

- ◆ Learning Activity 11–8: Writing SMART Objectives

- ◆ Learning Activity 11–9: Applying the Triple Constraint

- ◆ Learning Activity 11–10: Identifying Project Stakeholders

- ◆ Learning Activity 11–11: Project Stakeholder Good Twins and Evil Twins

- ◆ Learning Activity 11–12: Creating a Product or Service Context Diagram

- ◆ Learning Activity 11–13: Creating a Project Scope Diagram

- ◆ Learning Activity 11–14: Managing Project Risk

- ◆ Learning Activity 11–15: Creating a Work Breakdown Structure (WBS)

- ◆ Learning Activity 11–16: Planning Project Communications

- ◆ Learning Activity 11–17: Creating a Network Diagram and Calculating Critical Path (Party Exercise)

- ◆ Learning Activity 11–18: Creating a Network Diagram and Calculating Critical Path for Case Study

- ◆ Learning Activity 11–19: Project Execution Simulation

- ◆ Learning Activity 11–20: Creating a Personal Action Plan.

For the participants:

- ◆ Handout 11–1: What is Project Management?

- ◆ Handout 11–2: How I Used the Nine Knowledge Areas

- ◆ Handout 11–3: Post-Project Review Preview

- ◆ Handout 11–4: Quick and Dirty Project Assessment of Management Lessons

- ◆ Handout 11–5: Project Case Study

- ◆ Handout 11–6: Stakeholder Good Twins and Evil Twins

- ◆ Handout 11–7: Cryptogram Cards

- ◆ Handout 11–8: Cryptogram Solutions

- ◆ Handout 11–9: Personal Action Plan

- ◆ Training Instrument 11–1: Scoring Grid for Team Projects

- ◆ Training Instrument 11–2: Workshop Evaluation Form

- ◆ Training Instrument 12–1: Weighted Selection Criteria

- ◆ Training Instrument 12–2: Unweighted Selection Criteria

- ◆ Training Instrument 12–3: Forced-Pair Comparisons

- ◆ Training Instrument 12–4: Project Charter Worksheet

- ◆ Training Instrument 12–5: Priority Matrix

- ◆ Training Instrument 12–6: Inventory of Potential Stakeholders

- ◆ Training Instrument 12–7: Risk Identification Worksheet

- ◆ Training Instrument 12–8: Risk Priority Worksheet

- ◆ Training Instrument 12–9: Communication Plan

- ◆ Training Instrument 12–10: Post-Project Review.

CD Resources

Materials for this training session appear both in this workbook and as electronic files on the CD that accompanies this book. To access the files, insert the CD and look in its "PDF Files" directory for any handout, training instrument, or learning activity mentioned in this chapter. You will find more detailed instructions and help in locating files on the CD by referring to the Appendix, "Using the Compact Disc."

Sample Agenda: Two-Day Session

DAY ONE

8:30 a.m.   Welcome and Ice-Breaker for One- or Two-Day Session (25 minutes)

Display slide 9–1 as participants enter. Welcome them and indicate that you are going to start with a short project simulation designed to introduce the class and to start looking right away at some basic project management issues.

Introduce Learning Activity 11–1: Ice-Breaker Mini-Project for One- and Two-Day Session (chapter 11, page 157). This activity asks groups to work as mini-project teams to perform an information-gathering project that will allow each team to introduce others in the room. They will have a couple of minutes to strategize their approach and estimate the amount of time it will take to complete the information-gathering project. They will be scored on the basis of their success in achieving the goals of the project and their overall ability to deliver the information as quickly and as close to their estimated completion times as possible.

Show participants the scoring model you'll be using and indicate that they will have a chance to discuss the appropriateness of the model later.

At the end of the activity, tally scores and proceed to the introductions of the participants, making sure that every member is introduced.

8:55   Introduce Objectives and Agenda (10 minutes)

Show slides 9–2 through 9–4 and ask the participants to select the four objectives that are most important to them. (They will indicate their top four objectives in completing the Workshop Evaluation Form at the end of day two.)

Show slides 9–5 and 9–6 and discuss logistics for start and end times, lunch breaks, and breaks during the morning and afternoon sessions, using a flipchart page to record the information for reference throughout the workshop.

9:05 Defining Project Management (25 minutes)

Show slides 9–7 and 9–8 to introduce the definition of a project, using the PMBOK definition of "project" as the starting point. Walk the participants through the chart on slide 9–8 that analyzes the terms used with the idea of differentiating between projects versus processes (ongoing activities that have no end). Also point out that projects produce something (products or services—as well as such things as documentation or training). Show slide 9–9. Explain that now that they have a preliminary definition of "project," they will begin to create a working definition of "project management."

Introduce Learning Activity 11–2: Defining Project Management (chapter 11, page 159).

9:30 Break (10 minutes)

9:40 The Nine PMI Knowledge Areas (10 minutes)

This activity introduces the role of the Project Management Institute in helping to improve the overall practice of project management. Show slide 9–10 and discuss how PMI has identified Nine Knowledge Areas, each containing important project management issues. Use slides 9–11 through 9–19 to briefly expand on each of these areas. (Depending on the audience, you should generally be able to move rather quickly through this material. Indicate that you are highlighting what could easily provide material for an M.B.A.!)

Show slide 9–20 and indicate that, although the discipline of project management contains a vast array of knowledge, workshop participants have probably already used most, if not all, of the knowledge areas in their previous work on projects.

Show slide 9–21, and introduce Learning Activity 11–3: Using the Nine Project Management Knowledge Areas (chapter 11, page 162).

9:50   Project Management Life Cycles (10 minutes)

Show slides 9–22 and 9–23 and indicate that projects typically are organized into phases collectively known as the Project Life Cycle. If you already have a life cycle defined for your organization, then this discussion does not have to take up a great deal of time. Show slide 9–24 and indicate that there are many different approaches to the Project Life Cycle and that organizations may choose one or several for managing projects. Usually the number of phases ranges from three to five, but there are many exceptions. PMI does not favor any one life cycle model over another.

Show slide 9–25. (If you already have a life cycle defined, you may want to substitute a slide with it.) Discuss briefly the purpose of each phase and ask participants for ideas about typical activities that would take place in each. Ask why it may be useful to use a consistent approach to managing projects within an organization by using a standard life cycle. Help conclude the discussion with slide 9–26, showing that by repeating the life cycle in future projects, project teams are able to apply valuable lessons from earlier projects, much as travelers become more proficient in navigating routes based on their past travels along the same highways. This is why the discussion during project closure of lessons learned is so important.

10:00   Post-Project Review Preview (25 minutes)

Leave slide 9–26 up and introduce Learning Activity 11–4: Post-Project Review Preview (chapter 11, page 164). Often it's useful to suggest that teams use an approach such as this not only at the end of the project but also as a way to get everyone "on the same page" at project launch, using their shared lessons as a foundation of best practices, mistakes to avoid, and risks that need to be managed for the current project.

10:25   Project Selection (10 minutes)

Show slides 9–27 and 9–28 to begin the discussion of project selection and initiation. Often project team members are not privy to the selection process, coming into projects only after they have been approved and funded. Today, more than ever, it's important to recognize that not every proposed project gets to see the light of day. This workshop introduces a couple of commonly used methods of project selection to serve as examples.

Show slide 9–29 to give some idea of the ways that projects come into being. Some of the "sacred cow" variety are selected because senior management favors them. Point out that some of the best projects may originate this way, especially when there are strong visionary leaders heading the organization. Other projects get selected because they show strong revenue potential, offer chances to save on expenses, offer better service, or increase competitive edge. Still others are mandated to manage organizational exposure to risk or to respond to new legislation or regulation.

Slide 9–30 makes the point that projects should be aligned with the stated mission of the business. Use the questions to get participants' responses about some of the examples on the slide—some obviously off base, others borderline at best.

Slide 9–31 provides some frequently used quantitative methods for selecting projects. Cover each point briefly, emphasizing the ones used most often in your organization. Indicate that participants will have a chance to practice using two examples from the list following the break.

10:35   Break (10 minutes)

10:45   Weighted and Unweighted Criteria (20 minutes)

Show slide 9–32, which shows a generalized form for computing weighted criteria. Indicate that for project selection, the cells across the top are for projects under consideration and the cells along the left side are for selection criteria. The second column is for entering scoring weights from 1 to 5, with 5 meaning most important, for each criterion. The small boxes in the upper-left corner of each cell of the matrix are for each project's score for a criterion, and the main portion of each cell of the matrix is for entering the weight times the score. Show slide 9–33 as an example of a completed weighted criteria scoring grid and make sure participants follow the method of computing each project's score.

Show slide 9–34 and explain that the unweighted criteria grid is very similar except that every criterion gets equal weight. The example, in fact, uses the same scores as the preceding slide but omits the weight.

Introduce Learning Activity 11–5: Weighted and Unweighted Selection Criteria (chapter 11, page 172) to give participants some hands-on experience using the two models.

11:05   Using Forced-Pair Comparisons (20 minutes)

Show slide 9–35 and indicate that forced-pair comparisons are valuable tools for ranking many kinds of items by priority, ranging from candidate projects to vacation destinations. Reassure the participants that the form, though daunting in appearance, is quite easy to use once they understand the process. Display slide 9-36 and discuss the six steps briefly before moving on to the example, starting with slide 9–37. Point out that the example here uses only seven items and that there is no rule about how many or how few items can be given priorities with the tool. (Obviously, lists of more than 10 items will require a larger grid.) Complete the demonstration by displaying slide 9–39, which shows the list with priorities shown.

After showing slide 9–40, begin Learning Activity 11–6: Using Forced-Pair Comparisons (chapter 11, page 174).

At the end of this activity, indicate that this brings the workshop to the project definition phase, which will begin with the creation of the project charter.

11:25   Chartering the Project (15 minutes)

Display slides 9–41 and 9–42 to introduce the project charter. Emphasize that the charter is the document that gives approval for the project to proceed, based on the information it contains. Show slide 9–43 and emphasize that the charter is a communication tool and should provide the reader with a good grasp of what the project is about.

Show slide 9–44 and briefly describe each of the bullet points. Comment that the charter is an evolving document and that certain elements are likely to be updated as the project progresses, each time with any approved changes. Slide 9–45 shows a copy of Training Instrument 12–4: Project Charter Worksheet. (If your organization has a similar template, substitute it and adapt the following discussion points as needed.)

11:40   Introduction to the Case Study (20 minutes)

Still referring to slide 9–44, compare the completion of the charter to a scavenger hunt that requires the project team to obtain information from a variety of sources. To illustrate the process of initiating a project charter, introduce Learning Activity 11–7: Case Study Introduction—Beginning the Project Charter (chapter 11, page 176). Before breaking for lunch, ask participants to keep their partially completed Project Charter Worksheets, which you will help them expand upon when they return.

Noon   Lunch Break (60 minutes)

1:00 p.m.   Writing SMART objectives (20 minutes)

With slide 9–45 still displaying, welcome back the participants from the lunch break and ask for any questions about the material so far, including the case study and the charter. At this point there may be some specific questions about the case study. The next activities will help further define the case and the project as the charter becomes more complete.

Show slide 9–46. Describe SMART objectives, covering each of the five elements:

1. Objectives should be stated in terms that include some quantitative target for the end product.

2. There should be some way of actually testing whether the stated target has been met.

3. The desired objective must be one that is actually possible to achieve within the time and cost parameters provided.

4. The desired objective should relate directly to the organization's business needs and stated mission.

5. The boundaries for completion date of the desired objective should be either a specific date or time or an "offset" from the beginning of the project. (For example, "must be completed within five months of project launch.")

Conduct Learning Activity 11–8: Writing SMART Objectives (chapter 11, page 178) to provide practice in applying the SMART criteria to project objectives. Ask to what extent these criteria help clarify the requirements of the project and project scope.

1:20   Stating Assumptions (10 minutes)

Slide 9–47 shows two graphics: one of a mind-reading psychic (enclosed in the universal "no" symbol) and a scribe. It may be impossible to capture every assumption people may have about the project, but the project charter should capture as many important ones as is feasible. Ask participants for some assumptions for the case study that they think would be important to document. Write a few on the flipchart and ask them to come up with at least one more for their team's Project Charter Worksheet.

1:30   Applying the Triple Constraint (15 minutes)

The project objectives and assumptions are two of the most fundamental activities that occur during the writing of the project charter. Another important part of the charter is the statement of project constraints. Constraints are any pre-established requirements that affect how the project is to be completed. Show slide 9–48 as you describe the most common constraints that affect projects: time, cost, and quality or scope. Satisfaction with the third constraint could be defined as meeting the stated requirements for the project, but in any case the third constraint involves the amount of effort put into the project or the number of features delivered. Some people formally refer to these three elements as "the Triple Constraint." Others prefer the informal "fast/cheap/good." A shoe repair shop owner was reminding customers of the three constraints with his sign that read "Time, Money, Quality: Pick any two."

As you display slide 9–49, explain how the Triple Constraint inevitably requires trade-offs. If one constraint changes, one or both of the other two elements must change as well. Ask for examples of such trade-offs that the participants may have experienced either in projects or in their own personal experiences.

Slide 9–50 illustrates a recommended project tool: the priority matrix. This simple form requires the project sponsor and stakeholders to agree upon the relative priorities of each of the three constraints and to indicate any specific measurement. Go over the example provided on the slide. At this point, introduce Learning Activity 11–9: Applying the Triple Constraint (chapter 11, page 179) to provide practice in creating a priority matrix. Refer to the Project Charter Worksheet section on project constraints, pointing out that the priority matrix would become part of the project charter. Ask for any other possible constraints that might be added for the current case study.

Display slide 9–51 and point out that as the initial objectives, assumptions, and constraints become clearer, the project moves into the definition phase.

1:45   Project Stakeholders (15 minutes)

Slide 9–52 gives the PMBOK Guide definition of the term "stakeholders." Ask for comments on each of the four points covered. How broadly can project benefactor be interpreted? For instance, are there projects that have universal benefits or are some targeted to just a small group of beneficiaries? The project requestor and project team are more obvious candidates for stakeholders, but how often are others affected by projects left out until the project is under way? Ask participants for examples of stakeholder omissions that have created problems and how they currently identify potential stakeholders.

Slide 9–53 gives a checklist of places to look in identifying stakeholder candidates. The list should make it clearer that most projects have a more far-reaching impact than is usually thought. Make certain everyone understands how the roles listed on the slide might be stakeholders in a project. The main point is that the array of stakeholders is much broader than most people think and that it's important to identify those who need to be involved as early as possible in order to avoid misunderstanding and missed project requirements.

Use Slide 9–54 to introduce Learning Activity 11–10: Identifying Project Stakeholders (chapter 11, page 180). At the end of the activity, remind participants that the charter will continue to evolve and undoubtedly new stakeholders will be identified. What is most important is to get an early start so as many key individuals as possible are kept "in the loop."

2:00   Break (10 minutes)

2:10   Encouraging Positive Stakeholder Participation (20 minutes)

Emphasize that constructive stakeholder involvement is one of the key success factors for projects. It will be

important to manage stakeholder expectations throughout the project, but—just as important—it will be important to set expectations for stakeholder participation. Learning Activity 11–11: Project Stakeholder Good Twins and Evil Twins (chapter 11, page 181) addresses this issue. At the end of the activity, ask participants whether they would be comfortable defining stakeholder roles in the project charter. Ask if they have model descriptions available from previous projects that might be helpful if they needed to write such descriptions.

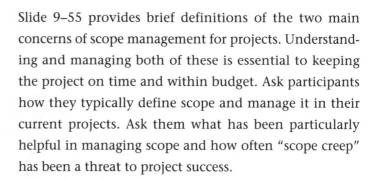

2:30   Defining Project Scope (10 minutes)

Slide 9–55 provides brief definitions of the two main concerns of scope management for projects. Understanding and managing both of these is essential to keeping the project on time and within budget. Ask participants how they typically define scope and manage it in their current projects. Ask them what has been particularly helpful in managing scope and how often "scope creep" has been a threat to project success.

2:40   Creating a Product Context Diagram (30 minutes)

One of the most powerful tools for defining scope is the scope (or context) diagram. The term "context" refers to the importance of defining a product or service at the appropriate level. Display slide 9–56 to illustrate the composition of the business areas of a fictitious organization called Widget World. In the example, you are trying to define a system to support sales—either as it currently exists or as it is to be after the project is completed (one can use Product Context Diagrams for both). The rest of the chart represents areas outside the context of supporting sales, so direct interaction with those areas would be part of the context diagram. Display slide 9–57 to illustrate a completed Product Context Diagram and point out the information flows to and from the product in relation to outside areas. Ask how some of the external areas help define the responsibilities and boundaries of the product. Slide 9–58 shows the components of a

Product Context Diagram. Point out that only four types of symbols are used.

Return to slide 9–56 and begin Learning Activity 11–12: Creating a Product or Service Context Diagram (chapter 11, page 183).

3:10   Break (10 minutes)

3:20   Creating the Project Scope Diagram (20 minutes)

Slide 9–59 shows a different kind of scope diagram, one for the project itself. This diagram depicts the main project at the center of the diagram, with entities external to the project as rectangles connected to it by arrows representing flows to and from the central project team. The symbols used in the Project Scope Diagram are nearly identical to those used in the Product Context Diagram and are shown on slide 9–60. Just as the Product Context Diagram helps define and contain product scope, the Project Scope Diagram is a powerful tool for showing the respective responsibilities of the project team and those outside the immediate team. Creating a good Project Scope Diagram is one of the first steps in setting and managing expectations throughout the project.

Use Learning Activity 11–13: Creating a Project Scope Diagram (chapter 11, page 184) to give participants a chance to apply their learning to the case study. After the activity, make it a point to commend the group for getting through some rather heady topics at the end of a long day.

3:40   Wrap-Up of Day One (20 minutes)

Assure the participants that they are nearly finished with the project definition stage. Point out that many of the steps taken so far have helped prevent some of the "gotchas" they identified in their post-project review preview. The tools and techniques covered so far help address project risks indirectly. Starting in day two, they will learn how to perform a formal risk assessment in order to even better manage threats to project success.

End the day by having participants jot down three or four of the most important new ideas they've obtained during the day and use a Koosh ball or other means to circle the room and have each member of the audience share something he or she learned.

DAY TWO

8:30 a.m.   Greeting and Review (15 minutes)

Welcome participants back for day two. Begin by informally reviewing the key materials from the preceding day. On a flipchart, aid the group in recalling the Nine PMI Knowledge Areas.

Then quickly review the phases of the life cycle used in the workshop (depending on the model you've decided to use). Ask for three selection tools used in the previous day (forced-pair, weighted, and unweighted scores). Finally, facilitate a brief discussion of the purpose of the project charter. Refer them to their copies of Training Instrument 12–4: Project Charter Worksheet (chapter 12, page 207) to determine the items that still remain to be addressed.

8:45   Project Milestones (5 minutes)

Indicate that at this stage the project phases themselves are useful milestones, but ask if the participants can identify any other useful milestones to note in the project charter at this time. Have them add any milestones identified to that section of the Project Charter Worksheet.

8:50   Assessing Risk (40 minutes)

Many of the steps taken so far in creating the project charter have helped to address such potential risks as unclear mission, scope creep, mistaken assumptions, and failure to agree on project priorities. It is now time to begin addressing other potential risks through a formal risk management process. All those "gotchas" from the past have shown us that the better we anticipate problems before they occur, the more likely we'll be to respond rationally and in ways that have the greatest chance of keeping our projects on track.

Show slide 9–61 to discuss how risks can be identified, given priorities, and managed. The slide shows Training Instrument 12–7: Risk Identification Worksheet (chapter 12, page 211) and provides explanations of each of its sections. Go over each of the items in detail, explaining that when we ignore a risk we decide to live with it and hope for the best (not a good idea if it's a serious threat). When we eliminate a risk, we generally change our direction to "detour" around it (for instance, we might avoid a technical risk by using a pen-and-paper solution). When we choose to manage a risk, we are making a commitment to take steps to anticipate, help prevent, and implement a contingency plan if the risk actually does take place. In other words, managing a risk costs time and effort—rather like buying insurance. We can't buy insurance for everything, so we have to carefully examine risks to decide which ones are the most threatening and must be managed. If we decide to manage a risk, we will take actions that would be logged to the Risk Identification Worksheet.

Show slide 9–62 to illustrate Training Instrument 12–8: the Risk Priority Worksheet (chapter 12, page 212). The version at the top shows the risks listed in the order identified. The version below shows the risks ranked in the order of priority. We need to remember that risk priorities may change as the project evolves or as circumstances outside the project change. (For example, air travel risks are considerably different now than they were a few years ago.)

Display slide 9-63 to introduce Learning Activity 11–14: Managing Project Risk (chapter 11, page 186). At the end of the activity, indicate that the project charter is complete except for the communication plan, which we will defer until we have initiated the project plan, in order to address all of the areas to be included in project communications.

9:30   Break (10 minutes)

9:40   Work Breakdown Structure (35 minutes)

Display slide 9–64 as participants return from the break. Indicate that we have now arrived at the phase of the project in which we will create the project plan and schedule. Show slide 9–65 to introduce the concept of the work breakdown structure (WBS). This is accomplished by using a technique of decomposing the project into manageable "chunks" that can be used to estimate durations, costs, and for assigning work to project team members or outside contractors. The two most common divisions are by project phase or product component. Show slide 9–66 to illustrate a WBS based on project phases. Slide 9–67, on the other hand, shows a large construction project that is deconstructed into major components. Point out that even the breakdowns on this slide are still at much too high a level for estimating and that further deconstruction would be necessary. Slide 9–68 defines Work Package as a lowest level of the WBS for a project. The Work Package may be divisible into lower-level activities, but those will usually be estimated separately as a subproject. The total estimates will then be reported back to the original project for estimating the main project.

Show slide 9–69 to explain that project activities can come initially either from higher level WBSs or can be done from the "bottom up" and then organized into logical groupings to create a WBS. At this point, introduce Learning Activity 11–15: Creating a Work Breakdown Structure (WBS) (chapter 11, page 188) to provide practice brainstorming and organizing activities into a WBS.

As organizations gain experience over time with similar projects, they generally are able to create project templates based on past projects in order to get a quick start on identifying activities for their current ones. Show slide 9-70 and discuss the pros and cons of templates. Caution the audience that templates are powerful tools but that they should never replace a thorough analysis of current project needs. The template should be a starting point, to be tailored as appropriate.

10:15   RACI Diagrams (15 minutes)

Display slide 9–71 to illustrate a high-level responsibility matrix (also known as a RACI diagram). The responsibility matrix is an indispensable tool for communicating various levels of involvement in the project. Have teams select four or five activities from their WBSs and determine who might be included on a full-blown RACI diagram. Discuss the value of having these charts available to others outside the project, such as the line manager of individuals assigned to the project. Point out how having RACI diagrams can help manage schedules and let others in the organization know when team members may be required for the project.

10:30   Planning for Communication (20 minutes)

Show slide 9–72 to introduce the concept of the Two-Floor Rule of project communications. The main premise of the rule is to keep everyone involved in the project up to date at the appropriate level of detail and to be ready at all times to provide information that is relevant to his or her particular role within the organization. You don't want to focus on the last file server downtime with the CEO unless that truly is the most relevant event at the moment—-probably not! Your team needs plenty of project details; your sponsor needs important financial data, updates on risks, and important milestones completed and pending. In order to keep all these levels of detail straight in an already over-burdened project manager's mind, a formal communication plan is a must. Show slide 9–73 to illustrate a typical example of a communication plan. Indicate that the participants may want to further detail each row on the plan in a paragraph or two, but at the very least they should consider using a grid like the one shown to organize their reporting. Introduce Learning Activity 11–16: Planning Project Communications (chapter 11, page 189) to provide practice in creating a communication plan.

10:50   Break (10 minutes)

11:00   Network Diagrams and Critical Path Analysis (15 minutes)

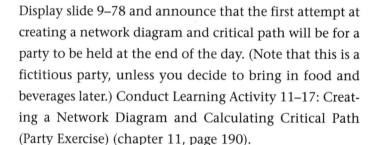

Display slide 9–74 as participants return from break. Having completed the project charter and the work breakdown structure, it is now possible to schedule the project. Indicate that scheduling normally starts by creating a network diagram. Show slide 9–75 and point out that two kinds of activities are used in developing schedules: the Activity on Arrow (AOA) and Activity on Node (AON). To illustrate each type of network diagram, show slides 9–76 and 9–77. These diagrams depict the same network of activities. (By the way, the Gantt chart logo on the bottom of each slide is actually a mapping of the same set of tasks and dependencies.) Point out the definition of critical path on both slides and walk participants through the calculation, making sure everyone follows the logic of why the path is "critical" to the completion of the project. Also make sure they understand where "slack" exists on the noncritical path.

11:15   Task Sequencing, Network Diagrams, and Critical Path (Party Exercise) (40 minutes)

Display slide 9–78 and announce that the first attempt at creating a network diagram and critical path will be for a party to be held at the end of the day. (Note that this is a fictitious party, unless you decide to bring in food and beverages later.) Conduct Learning Activity 11–17: Creating a Network Diagram and Calculating Critical Path (Party Exercise) (chapter 11, page 190).

Following the activity, display slide 9–82 and let the participants know that the diagrams included on the slides were created using a project management software tool (Microsoft Project). Reassure them that in real life they might not have to perform all the calculations used in the exercise but that it is highly recommended that they have a good grasp of what the software does. Far too often, project teams find themselves working with cost and schedule figures without understanding how they were derived. Project management software is a tool, nothing more. In order to further reinforce project scheduling concepts, everyone will have a chance after lunch to create a network diagram of the activities he or she created for the WBS in Learning Activity 11–15.

11:55   Lunch Break (60 minutes)

12:55 p.m.   Creating a High-Level Network and Critical Path for the Case Study (60 minutes)

As participants return from lunch, redisplay slide 9–79 as a model for the calculations to be performed in Learning Activity 11–18: Creating a Network Diagram and Calculating Critical Path for Case Study (chapter 11, page 192). Introduce the activity. Leave ample time at the end of the activity to debrief and share insights obtained in working through the activity. Ask participants if it gave them a better sense of how project schedules worked. See if they think that now that they understand the underlying principles they would be able to use a tool such as Microsoft Project to track and make changes.

Prior to the break, indicate that this concludes the planning phase of the project. Note that in addition to the plan itself, they already have determined how they were going to report progress, how they could manage risk, who was responsible for what tasks, and almost all areas of concern for managing a project. After the break, they will briefly examine some new tracking tools and then participate in one final project execution simulation.

1:55   Break (10 minutes)

2:05   Tools and Budget Issues (20 minutes)

Display slide 9–83 as participants return from break. Before the break, there had been a discussion of project management software. Now it would be worthwhile to look at a few "low-tech" solutions to tracking projects. All four of these tools are easy to implement and easy for those to whom you report progress to understand. They are all of the Two-Floor Rule variety. Show slide 9–84, the simplest of all reporting mechanisms. This could certainly be a standard weekly format for even the most overtaxed project team member. Ask what the advantages would be in using such a simple reporting tool and whether there are any risks in being *too* simple. Discuss what might slip through the cracks with this simple a tool.

Slide 9–85 presents a slightly more rigorous reporting tool. Because it is based on comparisons to the original plan, it works quite literally as a tracking tool. It is unblinking in its objectivity and for that reason is highly recommended.

Slide 9–86, the budgetary counterpart of the schedule milestone chart, has similar virtues. More sophisticated indicators are available, such as Earned Value calculations, but, as a minimum, this form can be incredibly useful.

Slide 9–87 reports the top five risks as of the reporting date. Recall that risks need frequent reevaluation. Using a regularly scheduled report such as this can serve as a reminder to revisit and reevaluate the risks that were identified in the planning process. Point out that new risks should be added during reevaluation.

Slide 9–88 is another important reminder to stay on top of project scope and the priorities of time, cost, and quality. If any of these change, it is almost always a sign of a major shift of project direction and may point to a reestimation of project plans.

2:25   Project Execution Simulation (45 minutes)

The activity to follow gives everyone another chance to plan and execute a project. The same scoring rules will apply as day one's first learning activity. However, this time there will be greater complexity in the project. Most project team members are involved in some form of multitasking or another, and Learning Activity 11–19: Project Execution Simulation (chapter 11, page 194) will help simulate the effect of multitasking on project team efficiency. Let participants know that the simulation will be followed by a short break and then proceed directly to the learning activity.

3:10   Break (10 minutes)

3:20   Project Management Training Close (10 minutes)

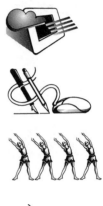

When participants return from break, display slide 9–89. Tell them that what they are about to see will look very familiar. Show slide 9–90, revealing the first page of Training Instrument 12–10: Post-Project Review (chapter 12, page 214). Remind participants that they built their learning over the past two days on some of the lessons they captured in Learning Activity 11–4: Post-Project Review Preview. Briefly walk through slides 9–90 through 9–93, pointing out the few differences between this and Handout 11–3: Post-Project Review Preview (chapter 11, page 166). Most notable is the final page, which contains a place for signatures. Ideally, projects should capture the lessons learned by all key participants and a formal presentation of findings as a major closure point for the project. Display slide 9–94 and point out that "Celebrate Successes" is not only recommended but ought to be mandatory. Each time through the process leads to further improvement. This is why the concept of continuous improvement has become an important part of the project management life cycle.

3:30   Project Management Maturity Model (5 minutes)

Display slide 9–95. One of the means for introducing continuous improvement is the Project Management Maturity Model (PMMM). Show slide 9–96 and give examples of organizational behavior at each level of maturity. Ask participants to do a quick mental check of where they are in the model and whether they are taking steps to improve. The fact that they are in this workshop is evidence of work toward attaining shared understandings. Some of the templates introduced are certainly signs pointing toward Level Three. Ask what else would be needed.

Show slide 9–97, which makes the promise of true project management magic: breaking the Triple Constraint through better, more efficient, repeatable processes.

3:35   Personal Action Plans (15 minutes)

Display slide 9–98. Point out that although you are about to end the class, this is just the beginning of what will be an exciting journey into the mastery of project management skills. Explain that the past two days helped build on previous experiences and allowed everyone to share ideas and practice a few new tools and techniques and that each person may have his or her own answers to the question to "what's next?" Display slide 9–99 and begin Learning Activity 11–20: Creating a Personal Action Plan (chapter 11, page 198). Conclude with the display of slide 9–101 before moving to the final activity of the day.

3:50   Final Words—Bibliography, Evaluations, Certificates (10 minutes)

Display slide 9–102 and open the floor for final questions, collect evaluations, issue certificates, and point to the bibliography in the back of the materials. If there is interest in any particular item, give your recommendation.

Congratulate everyone on completing the workshop and wish them *bon voyage* on their journey into the world of project management.

What to Do Next

Like its shorter counterparts, this two-day workshop may call for modifications to meet your organization's specific training needs. Perhaps you will want to add modules similar to the ones outlined in chapter 10. If so, consider omitting some of the topics presented; or use chapters 7 and 8 to get ideas for condensing some of the activities provided here. As always, you will find it helpful to meet with participants after the first few workshops for a mini–focus group to evaluate the content and determine what might be added or changed in "version 2" of your two-day offering.

Slide 9–1

Project Management Essentials

A Two-Day Workshop

Slide 9–2

Workshop Objectives

- Create a working definition of the term "project management."
- Identify the distinguishing characteristics of projects versus other processes in an organization.
- Employ commonly used techniques for selecting projects from a list of candidate projects.
- Determine how each of PMI's Nine Project Management Knowledge Areas can be used to improve project performance.
- Name the key stakeholders in a project and determine ways of keeping them "on task" during the phases of a project.
- Break a project into logical phases and specify the primary activities that occur in each phase.
- Effectively use the components of a project charter and appropriately scale each of them based on the size of a project.
- Write SMART project objectives that will help define project scope.

Slide 9–3

Workshop Objectives (continued)

- Document and clearly communicate project assumptions.
- Develop a procedure for managing changes in the project once it is underway.
- Create a Work Breakdown Structure (WBS) for a project.
- Sequence activities within a project based on mandatory and discretionary dependencies.
- Estimate activity durations and make appropriate adjustments as needed.
- Understand the role of "The Triple Constraint" in project management and apply it in determining project scope.
- Calculate the critical path for a project and develop a strategy for keeping the project on track.
- Differentiate milestones from other project activities and use milestones to help track and manage project progress.
- Identify, quantify, and give priorities to risks in managing a project.

Slide 9–4

Workshop Objectives (continued)

- Create a communication plan for reporting project progress and issues.
- Use tools for measuring project progress in terms of time, costs, and deliverables.
- Develop a strategy for managing project resources by using a responsibility matrix for assigning project activities to resources.
- Capture valuable project lessons learned and use them to define and improve project management practices within your organization.
- Develop an action plan for continuing to expand your project management knowledge.

Slide 9–5

Workshop Agenda—Day 1

1. Introduction: What Is Project Management?
2. The Project Management Cycle
3. Project Initiation
4. Project Definition

Slide 9–6

Workshop Agenda—Day 2

1. Planning and Scheduling the Project
2. Implementation: Project Execution and Control
3. Closure
4. Continuous Improvement
5. What's Next?
6. Bibliography

Slide 9–7

1.1—Introduction:
What Is Project Management?

Slide 9–8

What Is a Project?

"A temporary endeavor undertaken to create a unique product or service."*

to create	Has an intention to produce something (project "deliverables")
unique	One of a kind, rather than a collection of identical items
product	Tangible objects, but could include things like computer software, film or stage works
service	Might include the establishment of a day-care center, for instance, but not its daily operations.

*2000 PMBOK Guide (p. 4).

Slide 9–9

Your Turn: What Is Project Management?

- There are few, if any, definitive definitions.
- Project management knowledge is shared understanding of what it takes to deliver products and services effectively.
- Your definition should evolve and continuously improve with your knowledge and experience collaborating on projects.

Slide 9–10

PMI's Nine Project Management Knowledge Areas

1. Integration Management
2. Scope Management
3. Time Management
4. Cost Management
5. Quality Management
6. Human Resource Management
7. Communications Management
8. Risk Management
9. Procurement Management

Slide 9–11

#1—Project Integration Management

- Bringing it all together:
  - Building the project plan
  - Project execution
  - Integrated change control
- Project management "nerve center"

Slide 9–12

#2—Project Scope Management

- Staying Vigilant in Defining and Containing Scope throughout the Project
  - Project Initiation
  - Scope Planning
  - Scope Definition
  - Scope Verification
  - Scope Change Control

Slide 9–13

#3—Project Time Management

- Determining What Gets Done and When through:
  - Activity Definition
  - Activity Sequencing
  - Activity Duration Estimating
  - Schedule Development
  - Schedule Control

Slide 9–14

#4—Project Cost Management

- Planning for Resources
- Estimating Costs
- Creating the Budget
- Managing/Controlling the Budget

Slide 9–15

#5—Project Quality Management

- Quality Planning
- Quality Assurance
- Quality Control

Slide 9–16

#6—Project Human Resource Management

- Organizational Planning
- Staff Acquisition
- Team Development

Slide 9–17

#7—Project Communications Management

- Keeping Stakeholders Informed and Involved
  - Communications Planning
  - Dissemination of Information
  - Progress Reporting
  - Administrative Closure

Slide 9–18

#8—Project Risk Management

- Expect the Unexpected!
  - Risk Management Planning
  - Risk Identification
  - Qualitative Risk Analysis
  - Quantitative Risk Analysis
  - Risk Response Planning
  - Risk Management and Control

Slide 9–19

#9—Project Procurement Management

For Projects Using Outside Resources:
- Procurement Planning
- Solicitation Planning
- Solicitation
- Source Selection
- Contract Administration
- Contract Closeout

RFP's R Us!!

Slide 9–20

Where to Begin?

Look back over your previous project experiences.

Chances are, you've used a little of each of these nine areas already.

The PMBOK merely codifies them and attempts to give us a framework for understanding and applying project management knowledge productively.

Slide 9–21

Your Turn: What We Know Already

- Look back over your previous experience in project management
- How many of the nine knowledge areas did you use? (Probably all nine!)
- Take a quick inventory and point to your most successful application use of that knowledge area.
- Pick up at least one new tip from others right now!

Slide 9–22

1.2—The Project Management Cycle

Slide 9–23

The Project Life Cycle

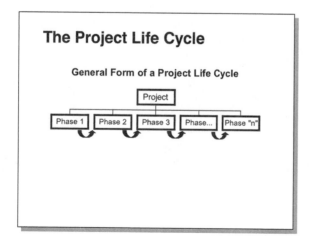

General Form of a Project Life Cycle

Slide 9–24

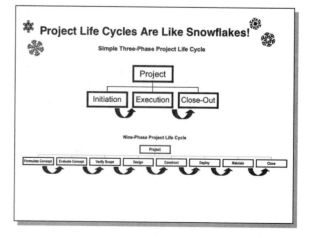

Project Life Cycles Are Like Snowflakes!

Slide 9–25

"Our" Project Life Cycle

Project Life Cycle Used in this Workshop

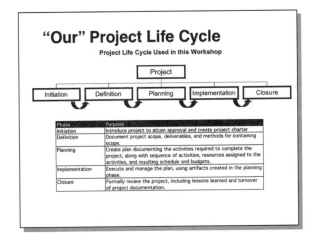

Phase	Purpose
Initiation	Introduce project to attain approval and create project charter
Definition	Document project scope, deliverables, and methods for containing scope.
Planning	Create plan documenting the activities required to complete the project, along with sequence of activities, resources assigned to the activities, and resulting schedule and budgets.
Implementation	Execute and manage the plan, using artifacts created in the planning phase.
Closure	Formally review the project, including lessons learned and turnover of project documentation.

Slide 9–26

Continuous Improvement

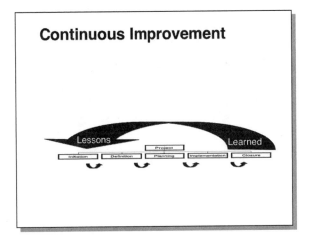

Slide 9–27

1.3 — Selecting and Initiating the Project

Slide 9–28

How Projects Come to Be

- Project selection can be a difficult process, especially when there are a large number of potential projects competing for scarce dollars.
- Some selection methods are highly intuitive; others try to add rigor through more scientific selection processes.

Slide 9–29

Sacred Cows and Pressing Needs

- "Sacred Cow" selection—Senior Management wants it! (It may often turn out well; many visionary projects start here)
- Business opportunity (make more $$$)
- Savings potential (save $$$)
- Keeping up with competition (example, many e-commerce projects were in response to competitor's initiatives)
- Risk management (examples (disaster recovery initiatives, Y2K)
- Government or regulatory requirements

Slide 9–30

First Selection Criterion

Sanity Check: Does the project fit in with the stated goals of the organization?

Which of the following meet this criterion? Why or why not?

- ❑ An environmental group proposes a project to raise money by selling aerosol cans of a powerful new pesticide.
- ❑ A video store chain proposes to develop a web site for ordering and distributing videos.
- ❑ A bank offers a free rifle to anyone opening a new savings account.
- ❑ A restaurant equipment manufacturer decides to introduce a line of high-end refrigerators for the consumer market.

Slide 9–31

Selection Tools

Numeric Method	Description
Payback Period	Determines how quickly a project recoups its costs
Net Present Value	Estimates the current worth of anticipated cash flows resulting from the project
Unweighted Selection	Scores multiple projects against a set of selection criteria, with all criteria being equal
Weighted Selection	Scores multiple projects against a set of selection criteria, with each criterion assigned a numeric weight
Pairwise Priorities	Rank ordering a number of candidate projects by systematically comparing one with each of the others

Slide 9–32

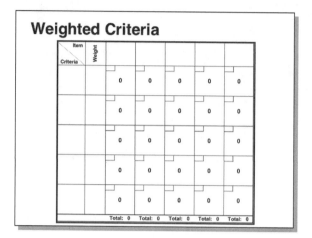

Slide 9–33

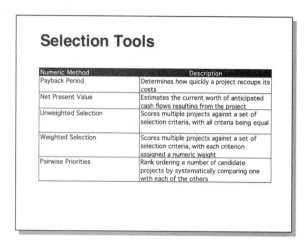

Slide 9–34

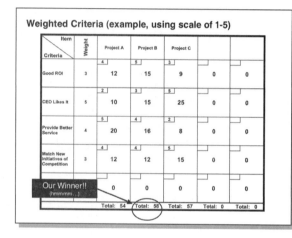

Slide 9–35

Forced Pair Comparisons for Priorities

- Allows individuals or groups to rank order lists of candidate projects (or anything, for that matter!)
- Simple
- Works well for fewer than 20 items

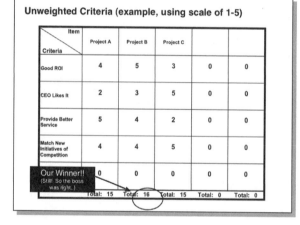

Slide 9–36

How to Use Forced Pair Comparisons

- Generate list of items.
  - For project selection, this will be the list of candidate projects.
- Number the items for identification purposes.
- Use the grid to compare each item with the other items on the list, circling the item that is the <u>more</u> preferred of the two. You must make a choice for each pair.
- Count the number of times each item was circled and enter its score on the bottom line of the grid.
- Rank order the list using the scores you have derived. The item with the highest score is number one. The item with the second-highest score is number two, and so on. In case of a tie, you may either do a mini-grid for the tied items or refer to your original preference when you were circling the items in the grid above.
- Use less than a full grid for fewer than 10 items; expand grid for more items.

Slide 9–37

How to **Use Forced Pair Comparisons**
Example:

Seven Books I've Always Wanted to Read and Haven't

1. Middlemarch
2. Ulysses
3. Remembrance of Things Past
4. War and Peace
5. Moby Dick
6. Anna Karenina
7. Pride and Prejudice

Slide 9–38

How to **Use Forced Pair Comparisons**
Example (continued):

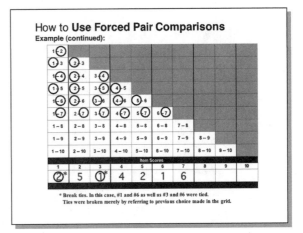

* Break ties. In this case, #1 and #6 as well as #3 and #6 were tied.
Ties were broken merely by referring to previous choice made in the grid.

Slide 9–39

How to **Use Forced Pair Comparisons**
Example (concluded):

Ranked List of the Seven Books I've Always Wanted to Read and Haven't

1. Pride and Prejudice
2. Ulysses
3. War and Peace
4. Middlemarch
5. Moby Dick
6. Remembrance of Things Past
7. Anna Karenina

Slide 9–40

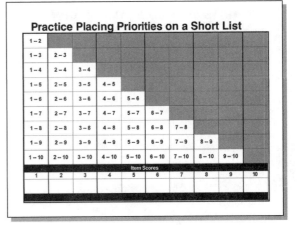

Slide 9–41

1.4—Chartering the Project

Slide 9–42

The Project Charter

- The project charter is the project's "license to do business."
- It should come from someone outside the project itself with funding-access, resource-assignment, and decision-making authority sufficient to support the project. This person is usually referred to as the project sponsor.

Slide 9–43

Why Have a Project Charter?

- Primary purpose: To get approval to proceed with the project and obtain sufficient approval for resources to move to the next phase of the project.
- Communicate to stakeholders and other interested parties the mission and the project's objectives.
- Communicate to the project team members what they are expected to accomplish.

Slide 9–44

Project Charter Components*

- Project Mission
- Project Scope
- Project Objectives
- Project Assumptions
- Project Constraints
- Milestones
- Project Risks
- Stakeholders
- Signature Page Granting Authority to Proceed

* In some organizations, the project charter is an evolving document. Many of the components listed will change as the project moves into the Project Definition Phase.

Slide 9–45

Your Turn: Starting the Charter

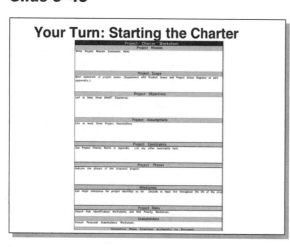

Slide 9–46

Writing SMART Objectives

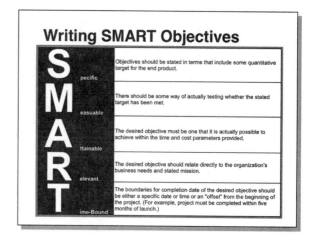

Slide 9–47

Project Assumptions

- Almost every lesson includes the reminder "Don't Assume!!"
- Turn that around and make it "Document Assumptions!"

  – Don't expect others to read your mind.
  – Capture as many assumptions as possible to include in your initial project charter.
  – Don't be surprised if others do not share all your assumptions. This is the time to resolve differences—<u>before</u> the project is underway!

Slide 9–48

The Triple Constraint

OR, IN PLAIN ENGLISH

Slide 9–49

Triple Constraint Trade-Offs

Time   Cost

Quality/Scope

Constraint Change	Required Adjustment Alternatives (One or Combination of	
Shorter Time	Higher Cost	Reduced Quality or Narrowed Scope
Reduced Cost	More Time	Reduced Quality or Narrowed Scope
Higher Quality or Increased Scope	More Time	Higher Cost

Slide 9–50

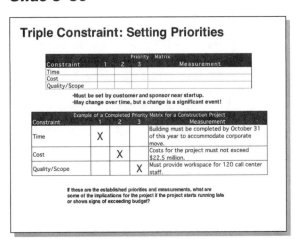

Triple Constraint: Setting Priorities

Constraint	Priority Matrix 1	2	3	Measurement
Time				
Cost				
Quality/Scope				

·Must be set by customer and sponsor near startup.
·May change over time, but a change is a significant event!

Example of a Completed Priority Matrix for a Construction Project Constraint	1	2	3	Measurement
Time	X			Building must be completed by October 31 of this year to accommodate corporate move.
Cost		X		Costs for the project must not exceed $22.5 million.
Quality/Scope			X	Must provide workspace for 120 call center staff.

If these are the established priorities and measurements, what are some of the implications for the project if the project starts running late or shows signs of exceeding budget?

Slide 9–51

1.5—Defining the Project

Slide 9–52

Project Stakeholders

- "Individuals and organizations that are actively involved in the project, or whose interest may be positively or negatively affected as a result of project execution or project completion." 2000 PMBOK Guide
- Short List
  - Project benefactor
  - Project requestor
  - Project manager and team
  - Those affected by the project

Slide 9–53

Project Stakeholders: Partial List of Candidates for Stakeholder Roles

- Project benefactor and upper management
  - Project Sponsor
  - Project Office/Project Advisory Boards
  - Executive Management
- Project requestor
- Project manager and team
  - If a team member has a line manager, he or she is a key stakeholder as well. (They hold the strings for your team member.)
- Internal Consultants
  - Legal
  - Audit
  - Telecommunications
  - IT Infrastructure
  - Quality Assurance
  - Human Resources Department
- External entities affected by the project
  - Customers
  - Vendors
  - Governmental agencies
  - Other regulatory bodies

Slide 9–54

Your Turn: Identifying Project Stakeholders

Potential Stakeholders
Stakeholders Inside the Team
Stakeholders Within the Walls the Organization
Stakeholders Outside the Organization

Slide 9–55

Defining Scope

- Product Scope Versus Project Scope
  - Product Scope: The sum of the features that make up the product or service created by the project.
  - Project Scope: All of the activities and resources required to produce the target product or service.

Slide 9–56

Preliminary Context Diagrams : Deconstruction

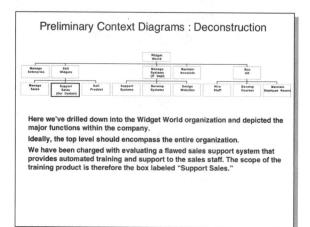

Here we've drilled down into the Widget World organization and depicted the major functions within the company.

Ideally, the top level should encompass the entire organization.

We have been charged with evaluating a flawed sales support system that provides automated training and support to the sales staff. The scope of the training product is therefore the box labeled "Support Sales."

Slide 9–57

Scope (Context) Diagrams
Defining the End Product

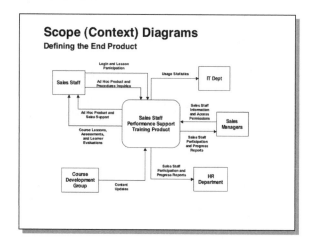

Slide 9–58

Scope (Context) Diagrams
Defining the End Product (continued)

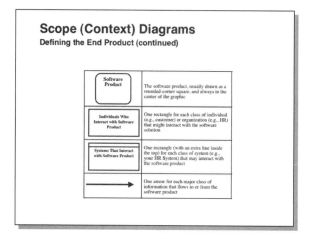

Slide 9–59

Scope (Context) Diagrams
(applied to project team charged with delivery of the product)

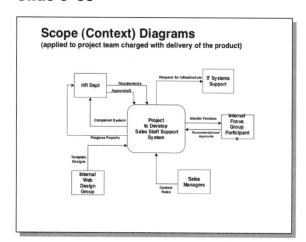

Slide 9–60

Scope (Context) Diagram
(applied to project team charged with delivery of the product - continued)

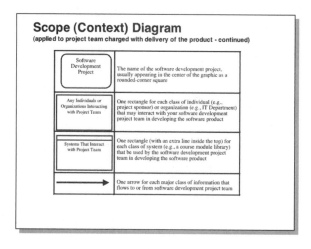

Slide 9–61

Risk Identification Worksheet

- Enter risk scenario (how an event could jeopardize project outcome).
- Rate probability, impact, and degree of control using rating scale of:
  - 1 = Low
  - 2 = Medium
  - 3 = High
- Compute risk index using formula:
  $$\text{Risk Index} = \frac{\text{Probability} * \text{Impact}}{\text{Control}}$$
- If possible, enter financial impact.
- Determine actions to take:
  - Ignore (do nothing)
  - Eliminate (sidestep)
  - Manage
- For managed risks, indicate mitigations and contingencies and assign risk manager.
- Log actions taken as they occur.

Slide 9–62

Giving Risks Priorities

Maintain inventory of all risks identified—updating probabilities, impacts, and controls if changes occur.

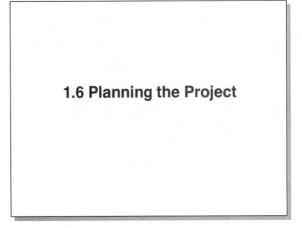

Focus attention on the risks with the highest indices.

* How would this change if you learned that a team member has announced that she is a finalist for a new position at the home office 1,500 miles away?

Slide 9–63

Your Turn: Project Risk Scenarios

1. Individually identify and jot down four possible risk scenarios that this project might face.
2. Share these within your group, and create a Risk Priority Worksheet of your pooled risks.
3. Score the risks.
4. For the top two, brainstorm at least one mitigation and one contingency.
5. Use the Risk Identification Worksheet as a guide, but you do not need to complete one for this exercise.

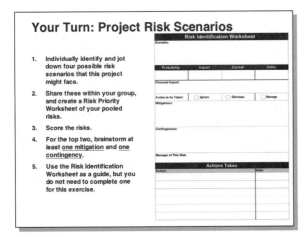

Slide 9–64

1.6 Planning the Project

Slide 9–65

Work Breakdown Structures

- Work Breakdown Structures (WBSs) help organize the activities required to meet the objectives of the project.
- Focus is on deliverables.
- May be organized:
  - By phase of the project
  - By component

Slide 9–66

Phase-Based WBS

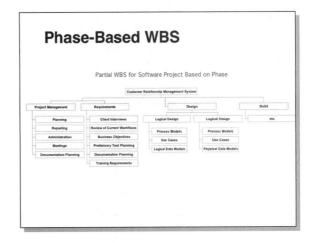

Partial WBS for Software Project Based on Phase

Slide 9–67

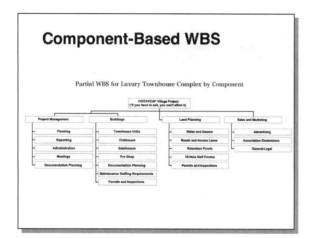

Component-Based WBS

Partial WBS for Luxury Townhouse Complex by Component

Slide 9–68

Work Packages

- The lowest level of WBS is called a Work Package if further deconstruction into activities is possible.
  - May be assigned as a subproject
  - May be subordinated into WBS structure for estimating purposes
- Activities at this level become the basis for time and duration estimates.

Slide 9–69

Sources of Project Activities: Brainstorming

Slide 9–70

More Sources of Project Activities: Templates

Don't reinvent the wheel!

- As you get more projects under your belt, work with other project teams to develop templates for WBSs to use as a starting point.
- Remember, no two projects are ever exactly alike (remember the "unique" in the definition of a project). The template should be a starting point—to be tailored to the specific needs of the current project.
- Even with the time spent in tailoring, templates can be enormous time-savers.

Slide 9–71

Assigning Responsibilities: Responsibility Matrix (also known as RACI Chart)

Cross-reference of tasks and resources assigned to the project.

Project Item	Sponsor	Project Manager	Project Team	Project Office
Project Definition	A	A	R	I
Risk Management	A	R	R	C
Detailed Design	A	R	R	C
Weekly Web Bulletin	I	R	R	I
etc.				

R =	Responsible
A =	Accountable
C =	Consulted
I =	Informed

Slide 9–72

Communication Made Simple

The Two-Floor Rule

 – Every stakeholder should receive information at just the right level of detail for them.
– High-level managers won't want to see all the gory details of the project.

 – Your team members need to see a great deal more.

 – If your level of reporting is appropriate, and one of your stakeholders steps into the elevator and asks about the status of the project, you should be able to brief him or her by the time the elevator stops two floors away.

Slide 9–73

Communication Plan

Communication	Format	Frequency	Distribution
Team Briefing	Restricted Intranet	Daily at 9:00	Team and stakeholders with access to secure project info area
Weekly Web Bulletin	Internal Intranet	Weekly	Team, sponsor, senior management
Technical Incident Report	Email	Immediately after Incident	Webmaster, IT Department
Budget and Schedule Detail	Spreadsheets and Detailed Gantt Chart	Bi-Weekly	Sponsor, Senior Management
Accomplishments and Setbacks	Email and Intranet	Weekly	All internal stakeholders
Schedule Milestones	Email and Intranet	Weekly	All internal stakeholders
Cost-to-Date Milestones	Email and Intranet	Weekly	All internal stakeholders
Current Top Five Risks	Email and Intranet	Weekly	All internal stakeholders

Slide 9–74

2.1-Scheduling the Project

Slide 9–75

Network Diagrams and Critical Path Analysis

Once you've determined the activities for the project and estimated their durations, network diagrams are the next step for the creating the project schedule.

Two Types:

    Activity on Arrow (AOA)—Nodes on the diagram connect arrows and represent activities.

    Activity on Node (AON)—Nodes represent activities that are connected by arrows showing the precedence of activities.

Slide 9–76

Network Diagram Example Activity on Arrow (AOA)

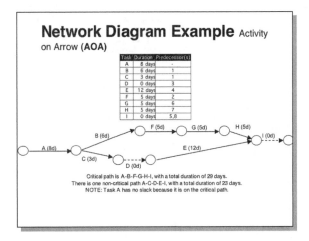

Critical path is A-B-F-G-H-I, with a total duration of 29 days.
There is one non-critical path A-C-D-E-I, with a total duration of 23 days.
NOTE: Task A has no slack because it is on the critical path.

Slide 9–77

Network Diagram Example Activity on Node (AON)

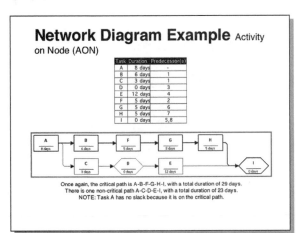

Once again, the critical path is A-B-F-G-H-I, with a total duration of 29 days.
There is one non-critical path A-C-D-E-I, with a total duration of 23 days.
NOTE: Task A has no slack because it is on the critical path.

Slide 9–78

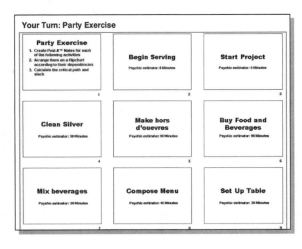

Slide 9–79

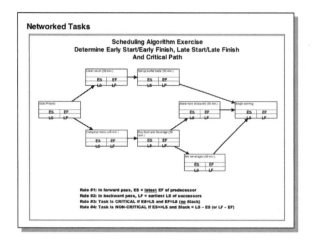

Slide 9–80

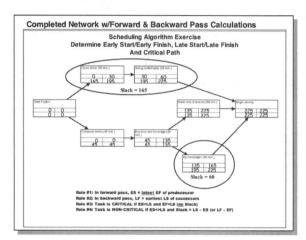

Slide 9–81

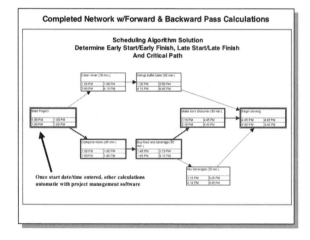

Slide 9–82

A Word About Tools

- Many people assume that project management is all about management software.

- That's like saying that residential construction is all about hammers!

- Such tools will often make your work simpler and handle complex calculations with ease.

- However, without a solid understanding of PM concepts, the tools often provide an illusion of project control that does not exist.

- Learn the concepts, then the tool.

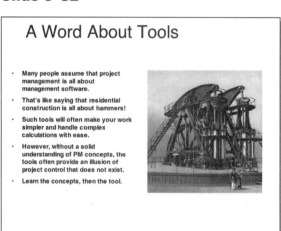

Slide 9–83

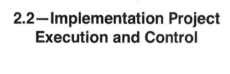

2.2—Implementation Project Execution and Control

Slide 9–84

Some Simple Tools

Accomplishments and Setbacks for Period Starting 2/9/04 – 2/15/04	
Accomplishments for Period	Setbacks for Period

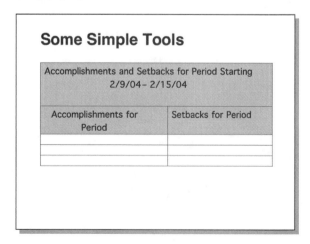

Slide 9–85

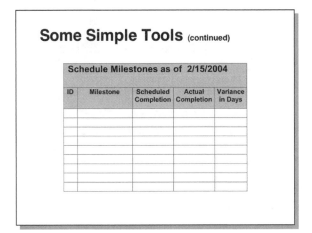

Slide 9–86

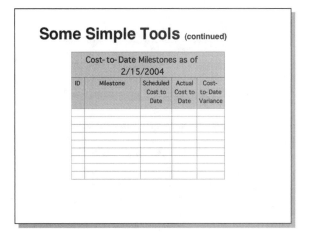

Slide 9–87

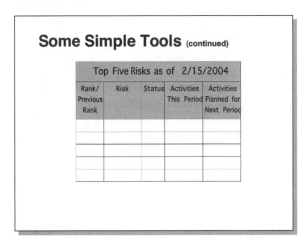

Slide 9–88

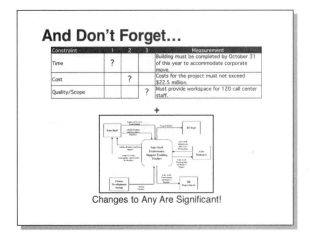

Slide 9–89

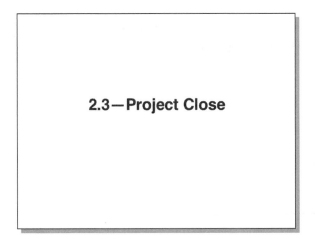

Slide 9–90

Slide 9–91

Post-Project Review (continued)

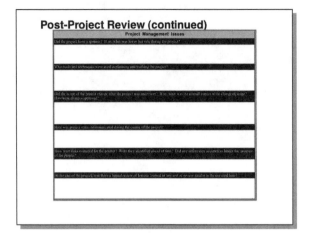

Slide 9–92

Post-Project Review (continued)

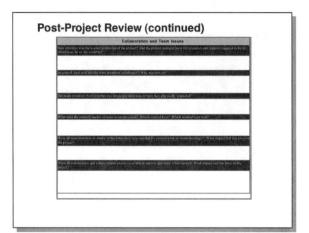

Slide 9–93

Post-Project Review (continued)

Slide 9–94

Stakeholders Report/Celebration

- Communicate Results
- Pinpoint Successes
- Propose Maintenance/Corrective Measures if Needed
  - share contributing success factors
  - present plans for corrective action
- "Sharpen the Saw" for Future Project Best Practices
- Celebrate Successes!

Slide 9–95

2.4—Continuous Improvement

Slide 9–96

Project Management Maturity Model (PMMM)

- PMI defines process improvement as the "Systematic and sustained improvement of processes and thus the products they produce."
- The five Levels of PMMM:
  - Level 1—Initial Process
    - Project management practices are ad hoc and inconsistent within organization.
  - Level 2—Repeatable Process
    - Project management practices are commonly understood and followed, but most knowledge is commonly understood rather than documented.
  - Level 3—Defined Process
    - Project methodology usually in place, with written guidelines for project deliverables and processes.
  - Level 4—Managed Process
    - Systematic collection of project performance data to set baselines for performance goals.
  - Level 5—Optimization
    - Proactive approach applying metrics and best practices to achieve highest level of project excellence.

Slide 9–97

Rewards of PMMM

The promise of continuous process improvement through repeatable processes, benchmarking, and optimization: To break the Triple Constraint and achieve

Faster!! Cheaper!!

Gooder, oops, Better!

Slide 9–98

2.5—What's Next?

Slide 9–99

Personal Action Plan

Personal Self-Evaluation and Action Plan for Follow Up after This Workshop
These are the knowledge areas and skills that I already knew and had reinforced by this workshop.

These are the knowledge areas and skills that were new to me. I will be able to use these in my project work in the future.

These are the knowledge areas and skills introduced in the workshop on which I might need a refresher in order to use comfortably.

Slide 9–100

Personal Action Plan (continued)

These are the knowledge areas and skills that I still would like to learn more about that were not covered (or not covered in sufficient detail) in the workshop.

Here are the steps I plan to take immediately

Here are the steps I want to take within the next 6 months

Here are any goals related to Project Management that I want to achieve within the next 2 years.

Slide 9–101

Personal Action Plan

- This plan is your plan and you need not share it with anyone else in the workshop.
- However, find a colleague with whom you can share your plan.
  - Make this "Project Management in the First Person" and set out to put in place the steps you listed to meet your stated goals.
- Much success in the future!!

Slide 9–102

Questions?

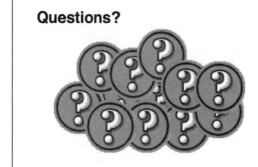

Slide 9–103

Bibliography

Slide 9–104

Bibliography

Adams, John R., and Bryan Campbell. *Roles and Responsibilities of the Project Manager* (4th edition). Upper Darby, PA: Project Management Institute, 1990.

Baker, Sunny and Kim. *The Complete Idiot's Guide to Project Management*. New York: Alpha Books, 1998.

Bennatan, E.M. *On Time Within Budget: Software Project Management Practices and Techniques* (3rd Edition). New York: Wiley, 2000.

Brooks, Fredrick. *The Mythical Man-Month*. Reading, PA: Addison-Wesley, 1995.

DeWeaver, Mary F. and Lori C. Gillespie. *Real-World Project Management: New Approaches for Adapting to Change and Uncertainty*. New York: Quality Resources, 1997.

Dinsmore, Paul C. *Human Factors in Project Management*. New York: AMACOM, 1990.

Doyle, Michael and David Straus. *How to Make Meetings Work*. New York: Jove Books, 1982.

Greer, Michael. *The Manager's Pocket Guide to Project Management*. Amherst, MA: HRD Press, 1999.

Greer, Michael. *The Project Manager's Partner: A Step-by-Step Guide to Project Management*. Amherst, MA: HRD Press, 1996.

Haynes, Marion E. *Project Management*. Menlo Park, CA: Crisp Publications, 1989.

Laufer, Alexander and Edward J. Hoffman. *Project Management Success Stories: Lessons of Project Leadership*. New York: Wiley, 2000.

Lewis, James P. *Fundamentals of Project Management*. New York: AMACOM, 1997.

Lock, Dennis. *Project Management* (6th edition). New York: Wiley, 1996.

Slide 9–105

Bibliography

Martin, Paula and Karen Tate. *Getting Started in Project Management*. New York: Wiley, 2001.

Meredith, Jack R. and Samuel J. Mantel, Jr. *Project Management: A Managerial Approach* (5th edition). New York: Wiley, 2003.

Penner, Donald. *The Project Manager's Survival Guide*. Columbus, OH: Battelle Press, 1994.

Peters, Tom, *Reinventing Work: The Project 50: Fifty Ways to Transform Every "Task" Into a Project That Matters*. New York: Alfred A. Knopf, 1999.

Project Management Institute. *A Guide to the Project Management Body of Knowledge (PMBOK Guide)* (2000 edition). Newtown Square, PA: Project Management Institute, 2001.

Roberts, W. *Leadership Secrets of Attila the Hun*. New York: Warner Books, 1987.

Schrage, Michael. *Shared Minds: The New Technologies of Collaboration*. New York: Random House, 1990.

Thomsett, R. *People and Project Management*. Englewood Cliffs, NJ: Yourdon Press, 1980.

Verzuh, Eric. *The Fast Forward MBA in Project Management: Quick Tips, Speedy Solutions, and Cutting-Edge Ideas*. New York, Wiley, 1999.

Wideman, R. Max, editor. *Project and Program Risk Management: A Guide to Managing Project Risks and Opportunities*. Newtown Square, PA: Project Management Institute, 1992.

Wysocki, Robert K., et al. *Building Effective Project Teams*. New York: Wiley, 2001.

Wysocki, Robert K., et al. *Effective Project Management*. New York: Wiley, 1995.

Topic Modules

◆ The list of the modules used in producing the workshops in this workbook

◆ Suggestions for adapting the modules

◆ Suggestions for adding new modules

The modules listed in this chapter are contained in the accompanying CD-ROM as a PowerPoint file, and are the basis for all of the PowerPoint presentations in the various versions of the project management workshops. The modules each cover a single topic and are intended to serve as the core of an expanding library for you to modify and expand upon as needed.

The module numbers are not intended to be indicative of any particular order of presentation. In fact, the higher module numbers usually indicate items added later in the development of the project management training library.

CD Resources

The modules listed here are available in a color PowerPoint verson as well as a black-and-white version for use in overheads and other non-color presentations. The modules are in a single PowerPoint file; however, you may wish to save these files separately for later use, if you find that the smaller individual files are easier to manipulate. You will find more detailed instructions and help in locating files on the CD by referring to the Appendix, "Using the Compact Disc."

Adapting Modules

You may wish to modify the existing modules to more accurately reflect your own organization's terminology or usage of forms and procedures. You may also wish to produce alternate versions of certain modules to add more depth of coverage for more experienced audiences, or to simplify some of the concepts for beginning project management students.

Adding Modules

Once you have the modules adapted to your purposes, you will want to begin to build upon the library and add new topics as time goes on. Keeping your materials modularized can make the process of producing new or revised workshops easier to manage.

The modules included on the CD are:

- ◆ Module 1: What is a Project?

- ◆ Module 2: PMI's 9 Project Management Knowledge Areas

- ◆ Module 3: The Triple Constraint

- ◆ Module 4: Risk Management

- ◆ Module 5: Project Selection

- ◆ Module 6: Work Breakdown Structures

- ◆ Module 7: Project Estimating

- ◆ Module 8: Project Stakeholders

- ◆ Module 9: Defining Scope

- ◆ Module 10: The Project Life Cycle

- ◆ Module 11: Project Management Software

- ◆ Module 12: Project Communications

- ◆ Module 13: Project Close

- ◆ Module 14: What's Next?

- ◆ Module 15: Bibliography

♦   Module 16: The Project Charter

♦   Module 17: Project Management Maturity Model

♦   Module 18: SMART Objectives and Project Assumptions.

What To Do Next

♦   Take time to look over the modules on the CD and prioritize any that need immediate revision to match your organization's project management practices.

♦   Note any topics you need covered that do not currently have modules and develop a timetable for creating them before time to roll out your project management workshop curriculum.

♦   Decide whether you want to keep the modules in one large file or break them down into individual files for later use.

Learning Activities and Training Instruments

This chapter contains the learning activities and training instruments used in the workshops on project management. The following are included, along with the handouts they require:

- Learning Activity 11–11: Project Stakeholder Good Twins and Evil Twins

- Learning Activity 11–12: Creating a Product or Service Context Diagram

- Learning Activity 11–13: Creating a Project Scope Diagram

- Learning Activity 11–14: Managing Project Risk

- Learning Activity 11–15: Creating a Work Breakdown Structure (WBS)

- Learning Activity 11–16: Planning Project Communications

- Learning Activity 11–17: Creating a Network Diagram and Calculating Critical Path (Party Exercise)

- Learning Activity 11–18: Creating a Network Diagram and Calculating Critical Path for Case Study

- Learning Activity 11–19: Project Execution Simulation

- Learning Activity 11–20: Creating a Personal Action Plan

- Training Instrument 11–1: Scoring Grid For Team Projects

- Training Instrument 11–2: Workshop Evaluation Form.

CD Resources

You will find the Training Instruments as PDF files on the CD included with this workbook. For more detailed instructions and help in locating files on the CD, please refer to the Appendix, "Using the Compact Disc."

What to Do Next

Take time to look over the materials here and note any that need immediate revision to match your organization's project management practices.

Note any topics you need to cover that do not currently have learning activities or handouts and develop a timetable for creating them before time to roll out your project management workshop curriculum.

Learning Activity 11–1: Ice-Breaker Mini-Project for One- and Two-Day Session

GOALS

The goals of this activity are:

- to introduce workshop participants to one another
- to demonstrate the estimation and completion of a mini-project
- to discuss models for evaluating project success.

MATERIALS

- Training Instrument 11–1: Scoring Grid for Team Projects
- flipchart and marker for instructor
- notepaper or Post-It notes for participants.

TIME

- approximately 25 minutes

INSTRUCTIONS

Let the participants know they will be working on a mini-project to gather information about the people in the room. When they have completed the project, each team should be able to introduce any person in the room* and provide the following pieces of information:

- name
- department and job title
- city of birth
- favorite movie
- what he or she considers to be the greatest project ever completed in history.

Each team will elect a project manager in any way they choose (often by whoever is slowest at pointing across the table!). The project manager and team will have three minutes to discuss their strategies for completing the project and will provide the facilitator with a "sealed bid" indicating how long it will take their team to complete.

On the flipchart, draw a copy of Training Instrument 11–1 and explain the scoring model:

The participants' final score will be their actual completion time plus half of the difference between their estimated and actual times. For example, if they estimate 10 minutes to complete the project and finish two minutes late (at 12 minutes), their score will be:

$$12 + (12 - 10)/2 = 12 + 1 = 13$$

If they estimate 10 minutes to complete and actually take only eight minutes, their score will be:

$$8 + (10 - 8)/2 = 8 + 1 = 9$$

After presenting the scoring model, give them their three minutes of strategy time and collect the "sealed bids" for the estimate.

Tell them "Go!" and note the lapsed time using Post-It notes on the top of the flipchart.

When a team completes the project, verify the following:

◆ they have collected all of the data

◆ they have included everyone in the room (including you).

Allow every team to complete the project if possible.

Assign each team to introduce the team at the table clockwise from them. Ask participants to stand when introduced so everyone can see them. Note any particularly interesting facts uncovered, especially about the project they thought the greatest of all time.

Debrief the project as follows:

◆ How was it like a real project?

◆ What worked especially well?

◆ What would they do differently if they were to conduct a similar project in the future?

◆ What do they think of the scoring model? (Why, for instance, is it fair to incur a slight penalty for completing early?)

NOTE: Most of the time, the participants will not realize that they are to include the facilitator as well in their information-gathering. This can provide a valuable lesson about assumptions in the debriefing.

Learning Activity 11–2:
Defining Project Management

GOALS

The goals of this activity are to draw on participant's intuitive understanding of the term "project management" and reach a shared preliminary understanding of the concept.

MATERIALS

- ◆ Handout 11–1: What Is Project Management?

- ◆ flipchart

- ◆ markers.

TIME

- ◆ approximately 25 minutes

INSTRUCTIONS

Instruct participants to write out their individual definitions of "project management" in the first section of the handout, asking them to use a single sentence—without bullet points. (Give them three minutes, but adjust time based on your reading of the group as they proceed with the assignment.)

Once they complete the individual definition, ask each team to appoint a coordinator in any way they see fit, "drafting" one of their members if necessary. Each team coordinator is to have each team member read his or her individual definition of project management and finally let the team hear the coordinator's own definition. Each team is then responsible for coming up with a composite definition of project management upon which they can agree—again without using bullet points or lists. Once they have their definition, they should transfer it to a flipchart page for discussion. Allow about five minutes for this activity. Each individual can retain his or her team's definition by using the second section of the handout.

Ask each coordinator to read the team definition from the flipchart, having each individual retain a copy of the definition by copying it into the third section of the handout. Discuss similarities and differences, emphasizing the strengths of each definition.

Indicate that the next step would be to consolidate the definitions into a single definition. Leave this as a possible homework exercise or ask participants to think about what that definition would look like and write out one sometime after the workshop.

Handout 11–1

What Is Project Management?

Instructions: In the space below, enter in your own words your definition of project management. Use a single sentence rather than a bulleted list.

Use this space for your team's definition of project management.

Use this space for the other teams' definitions.

After this workshop, create your own working definition.

Learning Activity 11–3:
Using the Nine Project Management Knowledge Areas

GOALS

The goal for this activity is to help participants recognize how PMI's Nine Project Management Knowledge Areas can be used to improve project performance by looking at how they have already successfully used this knowledge.

MATERIALS

- ◆ Handout 11–2: How I Used the Nine Knowledge Areas

- ◆ PowerPoint slides 8–8 through 8–10 for the one-day workshop

- ◆ PowerPoint slides 9–10 through 9–19 for the two-day workshop.

TIME

- ◆ approximately 15 minutes

INSTRUCTIONS

Distribute the handout and ask participants to use the form as a guide for jotting down where they have already used the knowledge areas. Indicate that they may not have used the knowledge in all nine, but that they more than likely have already had experience in a good many of them. Ask for some examples from each of the areas and if having these categories could be helpful in organizing their thoughts about managing projects and about attaining more project management expertise.

Handout 11-2
How I Used the Nine Knowledge Areas

Instructions: For each of the nine knowledge areas, look back over your past project experience and if possible pick a "defining moment," in which you intuitively used that knowledge extremely well.

1. Integration Management

2. Scope Management

3. Time Management

4. Cost Management

5. Quality Management

6. Human Resource Management

7. Communications Management

8. Risk Management

9. Procurement Management

Learning Activity 11–4:
Post-Project Review Preview

GOALS

The goal of this activity is to illustrate the applicability of lessons learned during a project and the value of the project review process.

MATERIALS

- ◆ Handout 11–3: Post-Project Review Preview

- ◆ Handout 11–4: Quick and Dirty Assessment of Project Management Lessons

- ◆ PowerPoint slide 7–9 for half-day workshop

- ◆ PowerPoint slide 8–15 for one-day workshop

- ◆ PowerPoint slide 9–26 for two-day workshop

- ◆ flipchart paper.

TIME

- ◆ approximately 25 minutes

INSTRUCTIONS

Indicate that the five-phase project management cycle shown in the first slide allows teams to improve the way they deliver projects with each new project they begin. This continuous improvement is only possible if project teams gather lessons learned throughout the project and formally review and document these lessons at the end of every project. Project closure has a number of other important activities, but none as important as that of making sure that the next project builds on the collective project experience of its team members.

Explain that the workshop will discuss the project closure in detail later but that the review process is so valuable that you'd like participants to experience first-hand the power of project reviews.

Distribute Handout 11–3 and ask each participant to complete all pages for the last project in which they participated either as a team member or a project manager. Ask participants who might be new to the organization to use any kind of project with which they have been associated, whether it was work-related, school-related, or related to a community activity, such as a picnic or other event. Ask participants to spend no more than a minute or so on each page and to limit the entire time in completing the form to five or six minutes—pointing out that in a real project review they would take greater pains to be thorough in answering each question.

Next, have participants each spend two or three minutes sharing their project history and lessons learned, using Handout 11–3 as a guide. (Caution: Make sure they understand that the handout is not to be read aloud but used as a reminder to help them share their stories.)

Once they have shared their stories, distribute Handout 11–4, indicating that the handout will be used later. For the moment, use the handout to create a shared flipchart page on which each team will quickly brainstorm "do's", "don'ts", and "gotchas", referring to the explanation of the three terms on Handout 11–4. Remind them that in brainstorming, quantity is preferable to quality. (Be prepared to defend this premise if necessary.) The team with the greatest total number of items in all three categories will be the winner of the round.

Rotate through the teams, having each team read its "do's", then "don'ts", then "gotchas"—leaving out any item another team has already mentioned.

Handout 11–3
Post-Project Review Preview

Instructions: Complete the following information for the last project in which you were involved, either as a team member or as an observer of the project.

The Project Itself

Write a brief description (50 words or less) of the project, its goals, its timeline, its approximate budget, and team members involved.

All in all, would you say that the project was successful? Why or why not?

How close was the project to meeting its scheduled completion date?

How close was the project to being completed within budget?

Did the project meet its stated objectives? Why or why not?

---

continued on next page

Handout 11–3, continued
Post-Project Review Preview

Project Management Issues

Did the project have a sponsor? If so, what was his or her role during the project?

What tools and techniques were used in planning and tracking the project?

Did the scope of the project change after the project was under way? If so, what was the overall impact of the change of scope? How were changes approved?

How was project status communicated during the course of the project?

How were risks managed for the project? Were they identified ahead of time? Did any unforeseen occurrences hinder the progress of the project?

At the end of the project, was there a formal process for gathering lessons learned or any sort of review similar to the one used here?

continued on next page

Handout 11–3, continued

Post-Project Review Preview

Collaboration and Team Issues

How effective was the overall leadership of the project? Did the project manager have the resources and support required to be as effective as possible?

In general, how well did the team members collaborate? Why was this so?

Did team members work together in a single physical area or were they physically separated?

What were the primary modes of team communication? Which ones worked best? Which ones worked less well?

Were all team members available at the times they were needed for project work or status meetings? What impact did this have on the project?

continued on next page

Handout 11–3, continued

Post-Project Review Preview

Were all stakeholders and subject matter experts available to answer questions when needed? What impact did this have on the project?

Technology and Knowledge Management Issues

How did technology help or hinder the progress of the project?

Were any new technology tools introduced for this project?

Did the project use any kind of project management software, such as Microsoft Project? In what ways was it used (for example, scheduling, reporting, or cost reporting)?

What other tools (for example, word-processors, spreadsheets, presentation software, diagramming tools) were used in the project?

continued on next page

Handout 11–3, continued
Post-Project Review Preview

Was the project team able to obtain adequate advice and technical support for the technology tools used in the project? How could this improve?

Are there any areas about which you would like to learn more that would make you more effective on your next project? What resources are available for obtaining that knowledge or skill?

Handout 11–4
Quick and Dirty Project Assessment of Management Lessons

Based on your group's discussion of your individual Post-Project Review Previews, brainstorm as many "do's" (best practices) as possible, which you'll want to carry forward into your next project.

Based on your group's discussion of your individual Post-Project Review Previews, brainstorm as many "don'ts" as possible, which you'll want to avoid in your next project.

Based on your group's discussion of your individual Post-Project Review Previews, brainstorm as many "gotchas" (unexpected surprises or setbacks) as possible, which you'll want to manage as risks in your next project.

Learning Activity 11–5:
Weighted and Unweighted Selection Criteria

GOALS

The goal for this activity is to apply weighted and unweighted scoring methods to selecting an item from a group of possible choices and to practice team decision making.

MATERIALS

- ◆ Training Instrument 12–1: Weighted Selection Criteria

- ◆ Training Instrument 12–2: Unweighted Selection Criteria

- ◆ PowerPoint slides 9–32 through 9–34

- ◆ plain paper

- ◆ flipchart paper.

TIME

- ◆ approximately 15 minutes

INSTRUCTIONS

Distribute the two training instruments and tell teams that in this exercise they have been asked to select a location for the next International Project Management Summit.

Important: The steps below should be performed in the order indicated.

1. They are to first come up with four or five criteria for selecting the conference site.

2. They then are to assign weights on a scale from 1 to 5 for each of their criteria, with the higher number always the more desirable.

3. Next have each team brainstorm five candidate cities and jot them on a piece of paper.

4. Next have each team pass their list on to the next team clockwise around the room.

5. Each team will then evaluate the five cities on the list they receive against the criteria that they themselves established in steps 1 and 2.

6. They then should transfer their grids to flipchart pages for sharing with the entire group.

Debrief the participants by asking what advantage, if any, there was in determining the criteria ahead of time. Also, see if any teams wound up with different selections in working with the unweighted selection model versus the weighted model.

Learning Activity 11–6: Using Forced-Pair Comparisons

GOALS

The goal of this activity is to provide practice using forced-pair comparisons in placing priorities on a list of items.

MATERIALS

- Training Instrument 12–3: Forced-Pair Comparisons

- PowerPoint slides 9–35 through 9–39

- plain notepaper.

TIME

- approximately 15 minutes

INSTRUCTIONS

Distribute two copies of Training Instrument 12–3 to each participant.

Indicate that learning forced-pair comparisons is fairly straightforward, but that it is complicated enough to make it worthwhile to practice more than once. Therefore, everyone will be generating two lists. Although this will be individual practice, encourage participants to share some of their top-rated items after each round.

Round One: The Impatient Genie

Tell the participants to take a piece of paper and pen or pencil. Describe the scenario as follows: "You have discovered a magic lamp and awakened the Impatient Genie. The genie will grant you seven things (not money or abstract concepts like happiness) that you can list within two minutes. Go!" (Give participants indicators of remaining time.)

Display the instructions slide (slide 9–36) again and then the example slide (slide 9–38) and assist anyone who needs help in completing his or her scoring.

Have participants share their top two items.

Round Two: The Witness Protection Program

Describe the second scenario as follows: "You are being moved to an undisclosed location, where you and your family will be provided housing, clothing, food, and furnishings. You will be allowed to take along only seven personal items." (Emphasize to participants that they will get such things as toothbrushes and that the seven items are presumably items that have sentimental or other value.) "You have two minutes to make the list. Go!"

Once again, ask them to share their top two items.

Learning Activity 11–7:
Case Study Introduction—Beginning the Project Charter

GOALS

The goal of this activity is to introduce the workshop's case study and to begin work in completing the project charter, writing a preliminary mission statement for the project.

MATERIALS

- Handout 11–5: Project Case Study

- Training Instrument 12–4: Project Charter Worksheet

- PowerPoint slide 8–21 for the one-day workshop

- PowerPoint slide 9–45 for the two-day workshop

- flipchart paper.

TIME

- approximately15 minutes

INSTRUCTIONS

Display slide 9–45. Distribute Handout 11–5 and Training Instrument 12–4 to each participant, and ask participants to take a few minutes to read the case study. Ask for questions and comments about the case, clarifying any items that are unclear to participants.

Indicate that for the time being they will only need to complete the first item on the training instrument: the project mission. Ask each participant to write his or her own mission statement of 50 words or less. Then ask each team to create a composite version on which they agree. Have them write their final version of the mission statement on the flipchart.

Handout 11–5

Project Case Study

Video Universe (VU) is a small chain of five video stores that rents and sells videos (VHS and DVD). VU caters to movie buffs who want to be able to request films by title, cast members, or directors, as well as look up Academy Award–winning films by category and year of award. Customers pay for rentals by cash or credit card. They may reserve a title up to five days in advance of the date on which they wish to rent. As a service, VU's main store has a conference room that it makes available to a local group of film buffs, who meet each week to discuss classic films available on video as well as notable new video releases.

VU's current file card–based system is inadequate for its needs and must be replaced. You are charged with analyzing the requirements, determining the scope of the system, and developing and implementing a plan to deliver the required system.

Managers determine rental pricing and acquisition information for new video purchases for inventory, which is purchased from one of several vendors. Data on films—such as cast and Oscar winners—comes from a subscription service, which provides the information monthly on CD-ROM. Cash receipts and credit card information are to be forwarded to the accounting group, which logs accounting information and handles collection of credit card transaction purchases. HR wants to receive reports on individual sales clerks for sales and rentals.

VU's owner is Sarah Sinema, who has indicated that she will make staff available to you and your project team if questions arise. Her staff of part-time sales clerks at the main store includes Sam Surly, Becky Belligerent, and Henry Helpful. Sarah has indicated that you may consult with any of them throughout the project. The main store also houses her accountant, Debbie Debit, and her HR director, John Hiram. Sarah has also suggested that you might want to meet with the weekly film group for ideas about how VU's new system might best serve their needs.

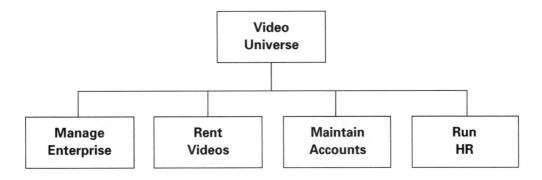

Learning Activity 11–8: Writing SMART Objectives

GOALS

The goal of this activity is to provide direct experience in writing project objectives that are specific, measurable, attainable, relevant, and constrained by time.

MATERIALS

- ◆ Handout 11–5: Project Case Study

- ◆ Training Instrument 12–4: Project Charter Worksheet

- ◆ PowerPoint slide 8–22 for the one-day workshop

- ◆ PowerPoint slide 9–46 for the two-day workshop

- ◆ flipchart paper.

Note: Both the handout and training instrument were distributed in an earlier activity.

TIME

- ◆ approximately 15 minutes

INSTRUCTIONS

Indicate that this activity should be collaborative. Ask each team to select a facilitator (rotate this responsibility from one activity to the next). The facilitator will be responsible for seeing that the team composes at least three SMART objectives, as outlined on the slide. Ask each group to use the SMART criteria as a checklist to evaluate their objectives. When they have completed their three SMART objectives, ask them to put them on the flipchart to share with the group.

As time allows, have teams read one another's objectives and evaluate them using the SMART criteria.

Learning Activity 11–9: Applying the Triple Constraint

GOALS

The goal of this activity is to provide hands-on experience in documenting and communicating project constraints and priorities of time, cost, and quality or scope.

MATERIALS

- ◆ Training Instrument 12–5: Priority Matrix

- ◆ Handout 11–5: Project Case Study (already distributed)

- ◆ PowerPoint slides 8–24 through 8–26 for the two-day workshop

- ◆ PowerPoint slides 9–48 through 9–50 for the two-day workshop

- ◆ flipchart paper.

TIME

- ◆ approximately 10 minutes

INSTRUCTIONS

Ask participants to work with their teams to complete the priority matrix based on the case study. Have them transfer their matrix to a flipchart page for sharing with the class.

Allow teams to take a minute or two to present their matrix. Point out that it will not be at all unusual for people to have different perceptions of priorities and that in a real project it would be important to reach consensus about the priorities before the project proceeded.

Learning Activity 11–10: Identifying Project Stakeholders

GOALS

The goal of this activity is to provide practice in identifying possible stakeholders for a project, given the current information available.

MATERIALS

- ◆ Handout 11–5: Project Case Study (already distributed)

- ◆ Training Instrument 12–6: Inventory of Potential Stakeholders

- ◆ PowerPoint slides 8–27 through 8–29

- ◆ PowerPoint slides 9–51 through 9–54

- ◆ flipchart paper.

TIME

- ◆ approximately 10 minutes

INSTRUCTIONS

Ask teams to review the project case study to identify possible stakeholders in each of the three categories on Training Instrument 12–6. Have them brainstorm additional candidates and post their categorized results on a flipchart page.

Circle the room and review the pages, noting similarities and differences.

Learning Activity 11–11: Project Stakeholder Good Twins and Evil Twins

GOALS

The goal of this activity is to help define stakeholder responsibilities in ways that will optimize stakeholder participation in projects.

MATERIALS

- ◆ Handout 11–6: Stakeholder Good Twins and Evil Twins

- ◆ PowerPoint slides 9–51 through 9–54.

TIME

- ◆ approximately 15 minutes

INSTRUCTIONS

Distribute Handout 11–6 and ask teams to decide which stakeholders they would like to use for this exercise. Individual team members will start completing the handout but may help one another in getting the best description possible of the Good Twin and Evil Twin behaviors. If people are stuck, suggest that they start with the Evil Twin behavior first, based perhaps on some experiences they've encountered in previous projects.

Ask teams to role-play the twins for presentation to the group, with "Oscars" for the best dramatic performances. Have each team deliver one Good Twin and one Evil Twin. After deciding on the most dramatic examples, move on to the role definition portion of the handout. How did the participants arrive at descriptions that would tend to encourage Good Twin behavior and discourage Evil Twin behavior?

Handout 11–6
Stakeholder Good Twins and Evil Twins

Stakeholder Name:

Pick one of the stakeholders involved in your project. Use the space below to indicate how that stakeholder's "Good Twin" would behave to help make your project an overwhelming success. Describe four or five specific ways in which he or she would do this.

Use the space below to indicate how that stakeholder's "Evil Twin" might behave to sabotage your project. Describe four or five specific ways in which he or she would do this.

Write a role description that could be included in a project charter to help ensure that the "Good Twin" would prevail over the "Evil Twin." (Strive for diplomacy here, please!)

Learning Activity 11–12: Creating a Product or Service Context Diagram

GOALS

The goal of this activity is to provide experiences in creating a product or service context diagram for defining product scope.

MATERIALS

- ◆ Handout 11–5: Project Case Study (already distributed)

- ◆ PowerPoint slides 9–55 through 9–58

- ◆ flipchart paper

- ◆ Post-It notes.

TIME

- ◆ approximately 15 minutes

INSTRUCTIONS

Depending on the audience, you may either create the context diagram as a facilitated presentation or as an exercise assigned to each team.

Refer to the slide 9–58, which shows symbols used in the diagram. Based on the participants' understanding of the requirements outlined in the case study, look at the decomposition of the organization and determine the area to be diagrammed. Place the rounded-corner symbol in the center of the flipchart and label it. Each outside entity should have a Post-It note. Arrange Post-It notes around the central symbol and determine high-level inflows and outflows of information to and from the other entities. *Important:* There are *no* arrows *between* entities. Those interactions are out of scope.

If there is no direct connection between an entity and the central symbol, then it too is out of context. Note that it is useful to retain any items identified as potential items for the diagram. A connection may be identified later.

If each team has created a diagram, have each team present it and note any differences. These differences in a real project would need to be ironed out and consensus reached. Usually participants see immediate value in the diagram, but make sure everyone understands why it is important to reach as accurate a description as possible of product scope.

Learning Activity 11–13: Creating a Project Scope Diagram

GOALS

The goal of this activity is to provide experiences in creating a project scope diagram for defining the scope of the project itself.

MATERIALS

- Handout 11–5: Project Case Study (already distributed)

- PowerPoint slides 9–59 through 9–60

- flipchart paper

- Post-It notes.

TIME

- approximately 15 minutes

INSTRUCTIONS

Depending on the audience, you may create the project scope diagram either as a facilitated presentation or as an exercise assigned to each team.

Refer to the slide indicating symbols used in the diagram. In the Project Scope Diagram, the project itself becomes the rounded-corner symbol in the center of the flipchart, and should be labeled with the name of the project. The immediate project team would be inside the central symbol and stakeholders outside the team would generally be the outside entities. Each outside entity should have a Post-It note. Arrange Post-It notes around the central symbol and determine high-level inflows and outflows of information to and from the other entities. *Important:* There are *no* arrows *between* entities. Those interactions are out of context!

If there is no direct connection between an entity and the central symbol, then it too is out of context. Note that it is useful to retain any items identified as potential items for the diagram. There may be a connection that will be identified later.

If each team has created a diagram, have each team present it and note any differences. The project scope diagram helps define the roles and responsibilities of project stakeholders in providing critical inputs as well as the responsibility of the project team to provide important outputs (including the final product or service at the end!). In real projects any differences in understanding would need to be ironed out and consensus reached. Usually participants see immediate value in the diagram, but make sure everyone understands why it is important to reach as accurate a description as possible of project scope.

Learning Activity 11–14: Managing Project Risk

GOALS

The goal of this activity is to provide hands-on experience in identifying, quantifying, prioritizing, and developing strategies to manage risk.

MATERIALS

- ◆ Handout 11–5: Project Case Study (already distributed)

- ◆ Training Instrument 12–7: Risk Identification Worksheet

- ◆ Training Instrument 12–8: Risk Priority Worksheet

- ◆ PowerPoint slides 9–61 through 9–63

- ◆ flipchart paper.

TIME

- ◆ approximately 30 minutes

INSTRUCTIONS

Indicate that this will be a combination of individual and team effort. Distribute copies of Training Instrument 12–7: Risk Identification Worksheet and Training Instrument 12–8: Risk Priority Worksheet.

Slides 9–61 and 9–62 provide guidelines for listing, scoring, and prioritizing risks. Display slide 9–63 as reference. The instructions on the slide say:

- ◆ Individually identify and jot down four possible risk scenarios this project might face. (Try to generate more if possible, but each individual should have more than one risk identified to add to the pool of risks brainstormed at the table.)

- ◆ Share these within your group, and create a Risk Priority Worksheet of your pooled risks. (Let each group have a few minutes to share the items they came up with. Then they should use Training Instrument 12–8 to enter the risks they've identified.)

- ◆ Score the risks. (If necessary, you can refer them to the example on slide 9–62.)

◆ For the top two, brainstorm at least one mitigation and one contingency. (The top two will have the highest scores. They can indicate how they might prevent the risk from occurring as well as what they would do if the risk occurred.)

◆ Use the Risk Identification Worksheet as a guide, but you do not need to complete one for this exercise.

Once the teams have completed the activity to this point, have each team put its top two risks on a flipchart page, along with their mitigation and contingency.

Have each team present their findings and similarities and differences. Ask for some additional risks that were identified in the process. Remind everyone that even the lower-priority risks should be maintained and periodically re-examined as the project progresses.

Learning Activity 11–15:
Creating a Work Breakdown Structure (WBS)

GOALS

The goal of this activity is to provide experience in brainstorming activities and in breaking them down and organizing them into a logical work structure.

MATERIALS

- ◆ Handout 11–5: Project Case Study (already distributed)

- ◆ Post-It notes

- ◆ flipchart paper.

TIME

- ◆ for the two-day version of the workshop, 20 minutes; for the one-day version, approximately seven or eight minutes

INSTRUCTIONS

For the two-day version of the workshop, teams should be expected to break down the case study into at least 20 activities. Using Post-It notes and flipchart paper, they should arrange the activities either by project phase or by major component.

For the one-day class, ask the teams to create a WBS either for one of the project phases or for just one of the components, depending on their choice of approach.

Have each team explain its approach and quickly enumerate the activities making up their WBS.

Learning Activity 11–16: Planning Project Communications

GOALS

The goal of this activity is to provide practice in creating a communications plan.

MATERIALS

- Handout 11–5: Project Case Study (already distributed)

- Training Instrument 12–9: Communication Plan

- flipchart paper.

TIME

- approximately 15 minutes

INSTRUCTIONS

Distribute Training Instrument 12–9: Communication Plan. Instruct each team to determine three or four major communications to implement during the execution of their project. Have them create a replica of the training instrument on their flipchart. Ask for a variety of formats, frequency levels, and target audiences. Give them seven or eight minutes to create their plans, and spend the remaining time comparing plans among the teams. Ask why they chose certain formats, what kinds of information would be on some of their choices, and how detailed it should be.

Stress the value of planning communications in advance and the urgency of maintaining the delivery schedule once they've established it. (Ask them why projects status reports often start falling behind. What does that normally signal? By the same token, what is usually implied by a sudden increase in reporting activity?)

Learning Activity 11–17: Creating a Network Diagram and Calculating Critical Path (Party Exercise)

GOALS

The goal of this activity is to provide practice in sequencing tasks, creating an AON network diagram, and calculating critical path.

MATERIALS

- ◆ PowerPoint slides 9–78 through 9–81

- ◆ Post-It notes

- ◆ flipchart paper.

TIME

- ◆ approximately 20 minutes

INSTRUCTIONS

The scenario is for a fictitious party that will involve the planning, preparation, and serving of food and beverages. The project will start at 1:00 p.m. The table setting would use some antique silver, which requires polishing. Food and drinks must be planned, bought, and prepared prior to starting the party. Indicate that the network diagram to be used is an AON (activity on node) and display slide 9–78 with the tasks. (You may alternatively want to brainstorm the tasks by hiding the slide and facilitating the tasks used in the exercise, but you'll want to wind up with the same tasks to be consistent with the presentation materials.)

Have each team create Post-It notes for each task and determine dependencies. One task is dependent on another if the other task must be completed first. For instance, for a new office we would wax the floor before moving in the furniture. Thus, moving the furniture is dependent on waxing the floor completing. (In fact, here there is another dependency: allowing the wax to dry!)

After determining dependencies, have participants arrange the tasks on a flipchart page with arrows depicting the dependencies. Have them pencil in the durations on each task.

Show slide 9–79, which contains the sample interim solution for the network.

Next, use slide 9–80 (animated to simulate filling in the times) to explain the concept of forward and backward pass for calculating critical path. Using the animation, walk the participants through the forward pass times, asking them to post the Early Start and Early Finish times and following the rules outlined on the slide.

Next have them work backward, filling in the Late Finish and Late Start times for each task, following the rules on the slide. Leave up slide 9–80, with all figures filled in. Note the circled areas around the non-critical tasks.

The final slide, 9–81, reveals the network with all items filled in, including the 1:00 p.m start time. (This illustrates the typical way that project networks are displayed. Project management software automatically calculates task times once the project start time is entered.)

Often, a second time through this exercise helps to reinforce the calculation methods. If time allows, suggest that they repeat the exercise as a "speed drill."

Learning Activity 11–18:
Creating a Network Diagram and Calculating
Critical Path for Case Study

GOALS

The goal of this activity is to apply network diagramming and critical path calculation to a more complex project: the case study.

MATERIALS

- ◆ Handout 11–5: Project Case Study (already distributed)

- ◆ Work breakdown structures created in Learning Activity 11–15

- ◆ Post-It notes

- ◆ flipchart paper.

TIME

- ◆ approximately 60 minutes

INSTRUCTIONS

This exercise will require a great deal of assistance from the facilitator and should only be attempted after the completion of Learning Activity 11–15.

Each team should make new copies of the activities from the WBS onto fresh Post-It notes, preserving their earlier WBSs for cross reference. Next they should perform a rough estimate of each task's duration (not being overly concerned with precision of estimates). After transferring the estimates onto each activity, teams will determine dependencies and create a network diagram, trying as much as possible to allow parallel activities to exist (just as they did in the "party exercise"). Have them include a milestone (zero duration) task for "Start Project" and for "End Project"

Often it is desirable to use a second Post-It note to place under each task with a grid for entering Early Start, Early Finish, Late Start, and Late Finish. Each task should be represented by a figure similar to those used for the tasks in the Party Exercise.

Have them determine task dependencies to create their network diagrams, just as they did in the Party Exercise.

Review their network diagrams to be sure they have included all tasks from their WBS and that the dependencies make sense.

Following the model of the party exercise, teams then would perform forward pass and backward pass calculations.. The same rules apply:

Rule #1: In forward pass, ES = latest EF of predecessor

Rule #2: In backward pass, LF = earliest LS of successors

Rule #3: Task is CRITICAL if ES = LS and EF = LS (no Slack)

Rule #4: Task is NON-CRITICAL if ES<>LS and Slack = LS – ES (or LF – EF)

Have teams highlight the borders of the critical tasks and pencil in the slack times for non-critical tasks. (See Rule 3 for Critical Tasks. See Rule 4 for Slack.)

Learning Activity 11–19: Project Execution Simulation

GOALS

The goal of this activity is to simulate a project once it is under way.

MATERIALS

For both the one-day and two-day workshops:

- ◆ Handout 11–7: Cryptogram Cards

- ◆ Handout 11–8: Cryptogram Solutions

- ◆ flipchart and marker for instructor

- ◆ notepaper or Post-It notes for participants.

In addition, for two-day workshop:

- ◆ 100-piece jigsaw puzzles for each team.

TIME

- ◆ 30 minutes for one-day workshop; 45 minutes for two-day workshop

INSTRUCTIONS

Each team will attempt to decode six encrypted messages. These are standard "daily newspaper" coding schemes, and most participants will be familiar with the concept. If not, take time to give a brief example. The goal of the project is to solve all six of the cryptograms.

For the two-day workshop, each team also will be expected to solve a relatively simple jigsaw puzzle.

Each team should elect a project manager in any way they choose (often by whoever is slowest at pointing across the table!). The project manager and team will have three minutes to discuss among themselves their strategies for completing the project and will provide the facilitator with a "sealed bid" indicating how long it will take their team to complete.

If you did not conduct Learning Activity 11–1, explain on the flipchart, draw a copy of the Training Instrument 11–1, and explain the scoring model:

Their final score will be their actual completion times plus half the difference of their estimated and actual times. For example, if they estimate 10 minutes to complete the project and finish two minutes late (i.e., at 12 minutes), their score will be:

$$12 + (12 - 10)/2 = 12 + 1 = 13$$

If they estimate 10 minutes to complete and actually take only eight minutes, their score will be:

$$8 + (10 - 8)/2 = 8 + 1 = 9$$

After presenting the scoring model, give them their three minutes of strategy time and collect the "sealed bids" for the estimate.

Tell them "Go!" and note the lapsed time using Post-It notes on the top of the flipchart.

When a team completes, verify that they have all of the crytograms solved.

Debrief the project as follows:

1. How was it like a real project?

2. What worked especially well?

3. How would they do it differently if they were to conduct a similar project in the future?

4. What do they think of the scoring model? (Why, for instance, is it fair to incur a slight penalty for completing early?)

Additional questions for the two-day workshop participants:

5. What was the effect of the multitasking of the cryptogram and puzzle?

6. How did you go about dividing up the work for the two parallel projects?

7. Do you generally think that multitasking is a good practice, based on your experiences in other projects and in this one?

Handout 11–7
Cryptogram Cards

EKSSWEE LE H SBXEWDKWXSW
HXY AKER XBR IW H CBHV.
(CKERHQW OVHKIWGR)

1

BVGGIBB CB GLVYXIW BDIIXIBX
UM XRLBI DRL YI'IP BVGGIIW.
(IOCHM WCGJCYBLY)

2

NZLBVIT EZWTR VR THFLXVR.
RVAATRR EZWTR VR KITTQM.
(EZRXH AXXBTM)

3

RHUUZRR CR WNPBZSJHR. JPZ
OZBCPR EJ UJTQ JPZRZVD, NPW
EJ UJTQ JPZRZVD CR IJSZ
WNPBZSJHR EYNP EJ UJTQ
JEYZSR.
(TNOVJ TCUNRRJ)

4

LTD LZSHTDFL LTQEH YRZSL
FSJJDFF QF LTYL NZS'PD HZL LZ
VDDB ZE RDQEH Y FSJJDFF.
(QOPQEH RDOMQE)

5

AWPI B VLETPF UXL OMZZPOO, B
UXLRXS SX EOC UXL OXMIF
OYPPV EIF RXXF FBRPOSBXI.
(HEOXI ZXXYPT)

6

Handout 11–8:
Cryptogram Solutions

Cryptogram 1
EKSSWEE LE H SBXEWDKWXSW
HXY AKER XBR IW H CBHV.

(CKERHQW OVHKIWGR)

Solution

Success is a consequence
and must not be a goal.

(Gustave Flaubert)

Cryptogram 2
BVGGIBB CB GLVYXIW BDIIXIBX
UM XRLBI DRL YI'IP BVGGIIW.

(IOCHM WCGJCYBLY)

Solution

Success is counted sweetest
By those who ne'er succeed.

(Emily Dickinson)

Cryptogram 3
NZLBVIT EZWTR VR THFLXVR.
RVAATRR EZWTR VR KITTQM.

(EZRXH AXXBTM)

Solution

Failure makes us envious.
Success makes us greedy.

(Mason Cooley)

Cryptogram 4
RHUUZRR CR WNPBZSJHR. JPZ OZBCPR
EJ UJTQ JPZRZVD, NPW EJ UJTQ JPZRZVD
CR IJSZ WNPBZSJHR EYNP EJ UJTQ
JEYZSR.

(TNOVJ TCUNRRJ)

Solution

Success is dangerous. One begins
to copy oneself, and to copy oneself
is more dangerous than to copy
others.

(Pablo Picasso)

Cryptogram 5
LTD LZSHTDFL LTQEH YRZSL
FSJJDFF QF LTYL NZS'PD HZL LZ
VDDB ZE RDQEH Y FSJJDFF.

(QOPQEH RDOMQE)

Solution

The toughest thing about
success is that you've got to
keep on being a success.

(Irving Berlin)

Cryptogram 6
AWPI B VLETPF UXL OMZZPOO, B
UXLRXS SX EOC UXL OXMIF OYPPV EIF
RXXF FBRPOSBXI.

(HEOXI ZXXYPT)

Solution

When I prayed for success, I
forgot to ask for sound sleep
and good digestion.

(Mason Cooley)

Learning Activity 11–20:
Creating a Personal Action Plan

GOALS

The goal of this activity is for participants to take away from the workshop a simple plan for expanding their project management knowledge and continue to improve project delivery throughout their organizations.

MATERIALS

- ◆ Handout 11–9: Personal Action Plan.

TIME

- ◆ 15 minutes

INSTRUCTIONS

It is important to make participants comfortable in doing this exercise. Assure them that they will not be expected to share anything that they write on their plans. However, encourage them to find someone either within the organization or among their friends and family with whom they can consult for encouragement and support in carrying out their plans.

Even though it is the end of the day, keep the room as quiet as possible, perhaps playing soft music to create a restful, soothing atmosphere. Provide indications of when there are only five minutes left, then give quiet warnings when two minutes and one minute remain.

When everyone is finished ask the participants to close their eyes for 30 seconds and try not to think of anything in particular. Then have them look to the front of the room for the concluding slide on Personal Action Plans.

Thank them for participating in this exercise and indicate your willingness to communicate with any of them about their plans after the workshop.

Handout 11–9
Personal Action Plan

Personal Self-Evaluation and Action Plan for Follow Up after This Workshop

These are the knowledge areas and skills that I already understood and had reinforced by this workshop.

These are the knowledge areas and skills that were new to me. I will be able to use these in my project work.

These are the knowledge areas and skills introduced in the workshop on which I might need a refresher in order to use comfortably.

These are the knowledge areas and skills that were not covered (or not covered in sufficient detail), but about which I would like to learn more.

These are the steps I plan to take immediately.

These are the steps I want to take within the next six months.

These are goals related to project management that I want to achieve within the next two years.

Training Instrument 11–1

Scoring Grid for Team Projects

Team	Project Estimated Duration	Project Actual Duration	Difference*	Score**

*Always use the positive difference between Estimated and Actual

** = Actual + (Difference)/2

Training Instrument 11–2
Workshop Evaluation Form

Workshop Date(s): _____

Your Name (Optional): _____

Department (Optional): _____

Workshop Objectives

Indicate the four workshop objectives that were most important to you and how well the workshop met those objectives. Also indicate how well in general you felt the other stated objectives of the workshop were met.

MY FOUR MOST IMPORTANT OBJECTIVES	VERY WELL	WELL	OK	BARELY	NOT AT ALL
1.	☐	☐	☐	☐	☐
2.	☐	☐	☐	☐	☐
3.	☐	☐	☐	☐	☐
4.	☐	☐	☐	☐	☐
THE REMAINING OBJECTIVES					
1.	☐	☐	☐	☐	☐
2.	☐	☐	☐	☐	☐
3.	☐	☐	☐	☐	☐

COMMENTS

	EXCELLENT	GOOD	FAIR	POOR
Overall Rating of the Workshop	☐	☐	☐	☐

WHAT WAS MOST VALUABLE TO YOU?

WHAT RECOMMENDATIONS WOULD YOU MAKE FOR IMPROVEMENT?

continued on next page

Training Instrument 11–2, continued

Workshop Evaluation Form

	EXCELLENT	GOOD	FAIR	POOR
Workshop Facilitator Rating	☐	☐	☐	☐
OVERALL FACILITATOR EFFECTIVENESS	☐	☐	☐	☐
FACILITATOR SUBJECT KNOWLEDGE	☐	☐	☐	☐
FACILITATOR PRESENTATIONJ SKILLS	☐	☐	☐	☐

WHAT DID YOU LIKE MOST ABOUT THE FACILITATOR'S PRESENTATION?

WHAT WOULD YOU RECOMMEND TO MAKE THE FACILITATOR'S PRESENTATION MORE EFFECTIVE IN THE FUTURE?

OTHER COMMENTS:

Project Management Training Instruments

♦ 10 training instruments for standard project management activities that are used in the workshops in this workbook

The following is a list of materials included in this chapter:

- Training Instrument 12–1: Weighted Selection Criteria
- Training Instrument 12–2: Unweighted Selection Criteria
- Training Instrument 12–3: Forced-Pair Comparisons
- Training Instrument 12–4: Project Charter Worksheet
- Training Instrument 12–5: Priority Matrix
- Training Instrument 12–6: Inventory of Potential Stakeholders
- Training Instrument 12–7: Risk Identification Worksheet
- Training Instrument 12–8: Risk Priority Worksheet
- Training Instrument 12–9: Communication Plan
- Training Instrument 12–10: Post-Project Review.

Training Instrument 12–1

Weighted Selection Criteria

Item / Criteria	Weight:					Total:
		□	□	□	□	□	Total:
		□	□	□	□	□	Total:
		□	□	□	□	□	Total:
		□	□	□	□	□	Total:
		□	□	□	□	□	Total:

Training Instrument 12-2
Unweighted Selection Criteria

Item / Criteria						
						Total:
						Total:
						Total:
						Total:
						Total:
						Total:

Training Instrument 12-3
Forced-Pair Comparisons

1—2										10	
1—3	2—3								9—10	9	
1—4	2—4	3—4						8—9	8—10	8	
1—5	2—5	3—5	4—5				7—8	7—9	7—10	7	
1—6	2—6	3—6	4—6	5—6		6—7	6—8	6—9	6—10	6	
1—7	2—7	3—7	4—7	5—7						5	
1—8	2—8	3—8	4—8	5—8						4	
1—9	2—9	3—9	4—9	5—9						3	
1—10	2—10	3—10	4—10	5—10						2	
										1	

Training Instrument 12–4
Project Charter Worksheet

Project Mission

Write project mission statement here.

Project Scope

Write a brief statement of project scope.

Project Objectives

List at least three SMART objectives.

Project Assumptions

List at least three project assumptions.

Project Constraints

List any constraints here.

Project Phases

Indicate the phases of the proposed project.

Milestones

List major milestones for project identified so far. (Include at least five throughout the life of the project.)

Project Risks

Attach Risk Identification Worksheets and Risk Priority Worksheet.

continued on next page

Training Instrument 12–4, continued
Project Charter Worksheet

Communication Plan

Attach copy of Communication Plan.

Stakeholders

Attach Inventory of Potential Stakeholders sheet.

Signature Page Granting Authority to Proceed

Obtain signatures of project sponsor and project manager.

Project Sponsor Signature: _____

Project Manager Signature:_____

Training Instrument 12–5
Priority Matrix

Priority Matrix

Constraint	1	2	3	Measurement
Time				
Cost				
Quality/Scope				

Training Instrument 12–6
Inventory of Potential Stakeholders

Stakeholders Inside the Team

Stakeholders Within the Walls of the Organization

Stakeholders Outside the Walls

Training Instrument 12–7
Risk Identification Worksheet

Scenario:			

Probability	Impact	Control	Index

Financial Impact:

Action to be Taken	Ignore ☐	Eliminate ☐	Manage ☐

Mitigations:

Contingencies:

Manager of This Risk:

Actions Taken

Action:	Date:

Training Instrument 12–8

Risk Priority Worksheet

Risk ID	Risk Scenario	Probability	Impact	Control	Index

Training Instrument 12–9

Communication Plan

Communication	Format	Frequency	Distribution

Training Instrument 12–10
Post-Project Review

Project Name: _____

Overall Evaluation of the Project

What was the overall mission of the project? Provide a short description based on your understanding of the project.

All in all, would you say the project was successful? Why or why not?

How close was the project to meeting its scheduled completion date?

How close was the project to being completed within budget?

Did the project meet its final stated objectives? Why or why not?

Project Management Issues

Did the project have a sponsor? If so, what was his or her role during the project?

What tools and techniques were used in planning and tracking the project?

Did the scope of the project change after it was under way? If so, what was the overall impact of the change of scope? How were changes approved?

How was project status communicated during the course of the project?

How were risks managed for the project? Were they identified ahead of time? Did any unforeseen occurrences hinder the progress of the project?

At the end of the project, was there a formal review of lessons learned or a review similar to the one used here?

continued on next page

Training Instrument 12–10, continued
Post-Project Review

Collaboration and Team Issues

How effective was the overall leadership of the project? Did the project manager have the resources and support required to be as effective as she or he could be?

In general, how well did the team members collaborate? Why was this so?

Did team members work together in a single physical area or were they physically separated?

What were the primary modes of team communication? Which worked best? Which worked least well?

Were all team members available at the times they were needed for project work or status meetings? What impact did this have on the project?

Were all stakeholders and subject matter experts available to answer questions when needed? What impact did this have on the project?

Technology and Knowledge Management Issues

How did technology help or hinder the progress of the project?

Were any new technology tools introduced for this project?

Did the project use any kind of project management software, such as Microsoft Project? In what ways was it used (for example, scheduling, reporting, or cost reporting)?

What other tools, such as word-processors, spreadsheets, presentation software, or diagramming tools, were used in the project?

Was the project team able to obtain adequate advice and technical support for the technology tools used in the project? How could this improve?

Are there any areas about which you would like to learn more that would make you more effective on your next project? What resources are available for obtaining that knowledge or skill?

Participant Name:_____

Participant Signature: _____

Evaluation Date: _____

CD Resources

You will find these materials as PDF files on the CD included with this workbook. For more detailed instructions and help in locating files on the CD, please refer to the Appendix, "Using the Compact Disc."

What to Do Next

Take time to look over the training instruments provided here and see if your organization has standard forms already in place to use instead of the generic training instrument. If so, plan to incorporate them into the workshops to better reflect practice within your organization.

Note any training instruments you would like to use beyond those provided and not already adopted by your organization. Investigate the possibility of developing them in conjunction with your organization's project management advisory staff.

Using the Compact Disc

Insert the CD and locate the file *How to Use This CD.*

Contents of the CD

The CD that comes with this workbook contains three types of files, designed to be used on a variety of computer platforms.

- **Adobe .pdf documents.** These include the Handouts and Training Instruments used in the workshops in this book.

- **Microsoft PowerPoint presentations.** These presentations have been designed to be an integral part of the workshops included in this book. The presentations have been designed to be as simple as possible to avoid competing with the sometimes complex content of a project management topic. In several cases the current background graphic has been suppressed to leave room for content material.

- **Microsoft PowerPoint files for overhead transparency masters.** These files are meant to be printed entirely in black-and-white without grayscale for any of the included graphics. (It is important to uncheck the "grayscale" box in the PowerPoint print dialogue box if your installation of PowerPoint automatically checks this box.)

Computer Requirements

You must have Adobe Acrobat Reader installed on your computer in order to print or view the .pdf files included on the CD. You can download Adobe Acrobat without cost from Adobe's Website, *www.adobe.com.*

To use or modify the PowerPoint presentation files on the CD, you will need to have Microsoft PowerPoint software installed on your computer. If you merely want to view the PowerPoint files, you will need to have one of a number of free viewers installed on your computer. Microsoft makes some of these viewers available for free download from its Website at *www.microsoft.com.*

Printing from the CD

TEXT FILES

To print the training materials using Adobe Acrobat Reader, open the desired .pdf file and print off as many copies as you need to prepare for your workshop. These are the .pdf documents that are available to print directly from the CD:

- ◆ Training Instrument 11–1: Scoring Grid For Team Projects

- ◆ Training Instrument 11–2: Workshop Evaluation Form

- ◆ Training Instrument 12–1: Weighted Selection Criteria

- ◆ Training Instrument 12–2: Unweighted Selection Criteria

- ◆ Training Instrument 12–3: Forced-Pair Comparisons

- ◆ Training Instrument 12–4: Project Charter Worksheet

- ◆ Training Instrument 12–5: Priority Matrix

- ◆ Training Instrument 12–6: Inventory of Potential Stakeholders

- ◆ Training Instrument 12–7: Risk Identification Worksheet

- ◆ Training Instrument 12–8: Risk Priority Worksheet

- ◆ Training Instrument 12–9: Communication Plan

- ◆ Training Instrument 12–10: Post-Project Review

- ◆ Handout 11–1: What Is Project Management?

- ◆ Handout 11–2: How I Used the Nine Knowledge Areas

- ◆ Handout 11–3: Post-Project Review Preview

- ◆ Handout 11–4: Quick and Dirty Project Assessment of Management Lessons

- Handout 11–5: Project Case Study

- Handout 11–6: Stakeholder Good Twins and Evil Twins

- Handout 11–7: Cryptogram Cards

- Handout 11–8: Cryptogram Solutions

- Handout 11–9: Personal Action Plan.

POWERPOINT SLIDES

You can print the presentation slides directly from the CD with Microsoft PowerPoint software by opening the .ppt files and printing as many copies as you'd like. You may create handouts using PowerPoint that display more than one "slide" per printed page. These may be printed in color or you may choose grayscale or black-and-white. (For best results for non-color, use the overhead masters file. The overhead masters correspond slide-for-slide with the color PowerPoint presentations, and most trainers today prefer to use an LCD projector to display the color versions of the slides during the workshop.)

Adapting the PowerPoint Slides

You may modify or customize the slides by saving a copy for the PowerPoint file from the CD and edit the copy. You are required to retain the denotation of the original source of the material—it is not legal to represent these materials as your own work. However, you may indicate that you have adapted your materials from the workbook, and indicate that it is from the book *Project Management Training*, written by Bill Shackelford and published by ASTD Press.

Displaying the PowerPoint Presentations

You will find the following four PowerPoint presentations on the CD:

- Half-Day Workshop.ppt

- One-Day Workshop.ppt

- Two-Day Workshop.ppt

- Modules.ppt.

If you double-click on a .ppt file, it will open in PowerPoint edit mode. However, if you right click, you may use the shortcut menu and select "Show," which will start the presentation in full-screen slide-show view, starting with the first slide in your presentation. (See Table A-1 for tips on navigating through a PowerPoint presentation.)

Work your way through the slide presentations several times to become familiar with the interface and to anticipate any "surprise" slides you may have forgotten. Some printer installations allow you to print as many as 16 slides on a printed page, and these can be helpful in providing you with a thumbnail map of your presentation. You may also wish to add speaker's notes to the slides, especially if you will be sharing presentation responsibilities with others in your organization. Speakers notes, the activity outlines provided here, and modular content materials will help you maintain consistency and reusability of training materials so that you may develop and maintain workshops more efficiently.

Table A–1
Navigating Through a PowerPoint Presentation

KEY	POWERPOINT "SHOW" ACTION
Space bar *or* Enter *or* Mouse click	Advance through custom animations embedded in the presentation
Backspace	Back up to the last projected element of the presentation
Escape	Abort the presentation
B *or* b	Blank the screen to black
B *or* b *(repeat)*	Resume the presentation
W *or* w	Blank the screen to white
W *or* w *(repeat)*	Resume the presentation

For Further Reading

Adams, John R. *Principles of Project Management: Collected Handbooks from the Project Management Institute.* Newtown Square, PA: Project Management Institute, 1996.

Adams, John R., and Campbell, Bryan. *Roles and Responsibilities of the Project Manager.* 4th edition. Upper Darby, PA: Project Management Institute, 1990.

Andrews, Dorine C., and Naomi S. Leventhal. *Fusion.* Englewood Cliffs, NJ: Prentice Hall, 1993.

Baker, Sunny, and Kim Baker. *The Complete Idiot's Guide to Project Management.* New York: Alpha Books, 1998.

Bennatan, E.M. *On Time Within Budget: Software Project Management Practices and Technique.* 3rd edition. New York: Wiley, 2000.

Brooks, Frederick P. *The Mythical Man-Month.* Reading, MA: Addison Wesley, 1995.

DeMarco, Tom, and Tim Lister. *Peopleware: Productive Projects and Teams.* 2nd edition. New York: Dorset House Publishing, 1999.

DeWeaver, Mary F., and Lori C. Gillespie. *Real-World Project Management: New Approaches for Adapting to Change and Uncertainty.* New York: Quality Resources, 1997.

Dinsmore, Paul C. *Human Factors in Project Management.* New York: AMACOM, 1990.

Doyle, Michael, and David Straus. *How to Make Meetings Work.* New York: Jove Books, 1982.

Ensworth, Patricia. *The Accidental Project Manager: Surviving the Transition from Techie to Manager.* New York: Wiley, 2001.

Gane, Chris. *Rapid System Development.* Englewood Cliffs, NJ: Yourdon Press, 1988.

Graham, Robert J., and Randall L. Englund. *Creating an Environment for Successful Projects: The Quest to Manage Project Management.* San Francisco: Jossey-Bass Pfeiffer, 1997.

Greer, Michael. *The Manager's Pocket Guide to Project Management.* Amherst, MA: HRD Press, 1999.

Greer, Michael. *The Project Manager's Partner: A Step-by-Step Guide to Project Management.* Amherst, MA: HRD Press, 1996.

Haynes, Marion E. *Project Management.* Menlo Park, CA: Crisp Publications, 1989.

Highsmith, James A., III. *Adaptive Software Development: A Collaborative Approach to Managing Complex Systems.* New York: Dorset House Publishing, 1999.

Kerzner, Harold D. *Project Management.* New York: John Wiley and Sons, 2001.

Laufer, Alexander, and Edward J. Hoffman. *Project Management Success Stories: Lessons of Project Leadership.* New York: Wiley, 2000.

Lewis, James P. *Fundamentals of Project Management.* New York: AMACOM, 1997.

Lock, Dennis. *Project Management.* 6th edition. New York: Wiley, 1996.

Martin, Paula, and Karen Tate. *Getting Started in Project Management.* New York: Wiley, 2001.

McConnell, Steve. *Software Project Survival Guide.* Redmond, WA: Microsoft Press, 1998.

McConnell, Steve. *Rapid Development: Timing Wild Software Schedules.* Redmond, WA: Microsoft Press, 1996.

Meredith, Jack R., and Samuel J. Mantel, Jr. *Project Management: A Managerial Approach.* 5th edition. New York: Wiley, 2003.

Modell, Martin E. *Data Analysis, Data Modeling and Classification.* New York: McGraw-Hill, 1992.

Penner, Donald. *The Project Manager's Survival Guide.* Columbus, OH: Battelle Press, 1994.

Peters, Tom. *Reinventing Work: The Project 50: Fifty Ways to Transform Every "Task" Into a Project That Matters.* New York: Alfred A. Knopf, 1999.

Project Management Institute. *A Guide to the Project Management Body of Knowledge, 2000 Edition* (PMBOK® Guide). Newton Square, PA: Project Management Institute, 2001.

Rad, Parviz F., and Ginger Levin. *The Advanced Project Management Office.* Boca Raton, FL: St. Lucie Press, 2002.

Roberts, Wes. *Leadership Secrets of Attila the Hun.* New York: Warner Books, 1987.

Russell, Lou. *Project Management for Trainers: Stop "Winging It" and Get Control of Your Training Project.* Alexandria, VA: ASTD, 2000.

Russell, Lou. *The Accelerated Learning Fieldbook: Making the Instructional Process Fast, Flexible, and Fun.* San Francisco: Jossey-Bass Pfeiffer, 1999.

Schrage, Michael. *Shared Minds: The New Technologies of Collaboration.* New York: Random House, 1990.

Shackelford, Bill. *Project Managing E-Learning.* Alexandria, VA: ASTD, 2002.

Thomsett, R. *People and Project Management.* Englewood Cliffs, NJ: Yourdon Press, 1980.

Verzuh, Eric. *The Fast Forward MBA in Project Management: Quick Tips, Speedy Solutions, and Cutting-Edge Ideas.* New York: Wiley, 1999.

Whitten, Neal. *Managing Software Development Projects: Formula for Success.* 2nd edition. New York: Wiley, 1995.

Wideman, R. Max, editor. *Project and Program Risk Management: A Guide to Managing Project Risks and Opportunities.* Newtown Square, PA: Project Management Institute, 1992.

Wood, Jane, and Denise Silver. *Joint Application Development.* New York: Wiley, 1995.

Wysocki, Robert K., et al. *Building Effective Project Teams.* New York: Wiley, 2001.

Wysocki, Robert K., et al. *Effective Project Management.* New York: Wiley, 1995.

About the Author

For the past 21 years **Bill Shackelford** has been president of Shackelford & Associates, a company specializing in training and development in project management, customer relationship management, information technology, business process training, systems design, systems development and support, and—for the past several years—e-learning. Shackelford's wide experience as a standup trainer has encompassed all major Microsoft operating systems and applications, including Microsoft Project, Web-based publishing design, database language products, object-oriented programming, project management, database

design, and data and process modeling. In addition, the company has developed systems ranging from membership management systems for a national association to a student financial aid needs analysis system to group insurance billing and receivable systems, and collection systems.

Major clients in legal, insurance, trade association, accounting, manufacturing, education, and PC training organizations have included the U.S. Department of Defense; Allegheny Power; Bank One; BP-Amoco Corporation; R.T. Nelson & Associates; Altrusa International; George M. Pullman Educational Foundation; Altheimer & Gray; American Association of Law Libraries; Keck Mahin & Cate; the Federal Reserve Bank of Chicago; Kemper Financial Services; The Hertz Corporation; The CIT Group; ChoicePoint; DiamondCluster; Northeast Utilities; Guilford County (NC); National Life of Vermont; Computer Generated Solutions; Conseco; Piedmont Natural Gas; Religious Science International; Penton Learning Systems; American National Educational Corporation; Books & Periodicals Online, Inc.; MicroAge, Inc.; Trade

Associates Group, Ltd.; Pannell Kerr Forster; Kenneth Leventhal & Co.; the state of Indiana; Transamerica; the Texas Department of Transportation; the state of Florida's Comptroller's Office; and the University of Texas.

PUBLICATIONS, PROFESSIONAL SERVICES, AND SEMINARS

Shackelford has served as editor and contributor to *Best Practices in IT Leadership* and has had articles published in the *Cutter IT Journal* and *T+D Magazine*. His November 2001 article on CRM and E-Learning was selected by Cutter Consortium for inclusion in its *A Practical Guide to Customer Relationship Management*. Shackelford served five terms as president of the Chicago Organization of Data Processing Educators. In May 2002, ASTD published Shackelford's *Project Managing E-Learning* as part of its E-Learning series. He has been a frequent speaker at seminars and conferences internationally, including OnLine Learning, OnLine Learning Europe, ASTD's International Conferences (2002 and 2003), Training 2003, DCI Conferences on Y2K, Data Warehouse, JAD/RAD, North American Simulation and Gaming Association, E-Learning Expo 2002, the 19th Annual Conference on Distance Teaching and Learning. Shackelford is a Phi Beta Kappa graduate of Indiana University, where he received both his bachelor's and master's degrees. Shackelford teaches both online and in the classroom on the faculty of the Keller Graduate School of Management in their Project Management M.B.A. program. An avid opera buff and Wagnerian, he is the Chicago correspondent for *Opera* (UK) and editor of the journal *Wagner News* of the Wagner Society of America.

ASTD Press

Delivering Training and Performance Knowledge
You Will Use Today and Lead With Tomorrow

- **Training Basics**
- **Evaluation / Return-on-Investment (ROI)**
- **E-Learning**
- **Instructional Systems Development (ISD)**
- **Leadership**
- **Career Development**

ASTD Press is an internationally renowned source of insightful and practical information on workplace learning and performance topics, including training basics, evaluation and return-on-investment (ROI), instructional systems development (ISD), e-learning, leadership, and career development. You can trust that the books ASTD Press acquires, develops, edits, designs, and publishes meet the highest standards for accuracy and that our books reflect the most current industry practices. In addition, ASTD Press books are bottom-line oriented and geared toward immediate problem-solving application in the field.

Ordering Information: Books published by ASTD Press can be purchased by visiting our website at store.astd.org or by calling 800.628.2783 or 703.683.8100.